# COUNSELLING AND PSYCHOTHERAPY WITH OLDER PEOPLE

# BASIC TEXTS IN COUNSELLING AND PSYCHOTHERAPY

Series Editor: Stephen Frosh

This series introduces readers to the theory and practice of counselling and psychotherapy across a wide range of topic areas. The books will appeal to anyone wishing to use counselling and psychotherapeutic skills and are particularly relevant to workers in health, education, social work and related settings. The books in this series are unusual in being rooted in psychodynamic and systemic ideas, yet being written at an accessible, readable and introductory level. Each text offers theoretical background and guidance for practice, with creative use of clinical examples.

*Published*

Jenny Altschuler
WORKING WITH CHRONIC ILLNESS

Bill Barnes, Sheila Ernst and Keith Hyde
AN INTRODUCTION TO GROUPWORK

Stephen Briggs
WORKING WITH ADOLESCENTS

Alex Coren
SHORT-TERM PSYCHOTHERAPY

Jim Crawley and Jan Grant
COUPLE THERAPY

Emilia Dowling and Gill Gorell Barnes
WORKING WITH CHILDREN AND PARENTS THROUGH SEPARATION AND DIVORCE

Loretta Franklin
AN INTRODUCTION TO WORKPLACE COUNSELLING

Gill Gorell Barnes
FAMILY THERAPY IN CHANGING TIMES 2nd ed.

Fran Hedges
AN INTRODUCTION TO SYSTEMIC THERAPY WITH INDIVIDUALS

Sally Hodges
COUNSELLING ADULTS WITH LEARNING DISABILITIES

Linda Hopper
COUNSELLING AND PSYCHOTHERAPY WITH CHILDREN AND ADOLESCENTS

Ravi Rana
COUNSELLING STUDENTS

Tricia Scott
INTEGRATIVE PSYCHOTHERAPY IN HEALTH CARE

Geraldine Shipton
WORKING WITH EATING DISORDERS

Laurence Spurling
AN INTRODUCTION TO PSYCHODYNAMIC COUNSELLING

Paul Terry
COUNSELLING AND PSYCHOTHERAPY WITH OLDER PEOPLE 2nd ed.

Steven Walker
CULTURALLY COMPETENT THERAPY

Jan Wiener and Mannie Sher
COUNSELLING AND PSYCHOTHERAPY IN PRIMARY HEALTH CARE

Shula Wilson
DISABILITY, COUNSELLING AND PSYCHOTHERAPY

**Invitation to authors**

The Series Editor welcomes proposals for new books within the Basic Texts in Counselling and Psychotherapy series. These should be sent to Stephen Frosh at the School of Psychology, Birkbeck College, Malet Street, London WCIE 7HX (email s.frosh@bbk.ac.uk).

**Basic Texts in Counselling and Psychotherapy**
**Series Standing Order ISBN 0-333-69330-2**
*(outside North America only)*

You can receive future titles in this series as they are published by placing a standing order. Please contact your bookseller or, in the case of difficulty, write to us at the address below with your name and address, the title of the series and the ISBN quoted above.

Customer Services Department, Macmillan Distribution Ltd.
Houndmills, Basingstoke, Hampshire RG21 6XS, England

# COUNSELLING AND PSYCHOTHERAPY WITH OLDER PEOPLE

## A PSYCHODYNAMIC APPROACH

SECOND EDITION

PAUL TERRY

*Birkbeck College, University of London*

First published 2008 by
PALGRAVE MACMILLAN
Houndmills, Basingstoke, Hampshire RG21 6XS and
175 Fifth Avenue, New York, N.Y. 10010
Companies and representatives throughout the world

PALGRAVE MACMILLAN is the global academic imprint of the Palgrave Macmillan division of St. Martin's Press, LLC and of Palgrave Macmillan Ltd. Macmillan® is a registered trademark in the United States, United Kingdom and other countries. Palgrave is a registered trademark in the European Union and other countries.

ISBN-13: 978–0–230–50654–1
ISBN-10: 0–230–50654–2

This book is printed on paper suitable for recycling and made from fully managed and sustained forest sources. Logging, pulping and manufacturing processes are expected to conform to the environmental regulations of the country of origin.

A catalogue record for this book is available from the British Library.

A catalog record for this book is available from the Library of Congress.

In memory of my dear friend and colleague Ellen Noonan

# CONTENTS

# Acknowledgements

I would like to express my gratitude to the older people and their carers who have contributed to this book. I would like to thank Grace Bartholomew the hospital manager, Pat Smiton the deputy manager, and Roger Ramsden the clinical psychology manager, for their unfailing support; my clinical supervisors and my analyst for enabling me to sustain and develop the work; and my current therapist for his enabling of this revision.

I benefited from organisational consultation with David Armstrong, then Director of the Grubb Institute; and the late Eric Miller at the Tavistock Institute of Human Relations.

I would like to thank my editor Stephen Frosh for his help in preparing this second edition. My late friend and colleague Ellen Noonan contributed generously when I was preparing the first edition and was a source of encouragement about the new material in this second edition. I want to express my thanks to my students and colleagues at Birkbeck College at the University of London with whom I have learned and continue to learn so much about counselling and psychotherapy.

I am very grateful to Dominik Ritter, Michele Cloherty and Gary Walker who were clinical psychology trainees on placement with me and who agreed to my drawing on experiences of supervision with them for the last chapter in the book.

The publishers and I are grateful to Dr A.H. Mann for giving permission to quote the words of the song *Danny Boy*.

Finally, special thanks to Philip Chklar for his continuing support.

# PREFACE TO THE SECOND EDITION

When I wrote the first edition of this book I was in my fifties and could still think of myself as young in comparison with my older clients. Ten years later this new edition brings a perspective from an older therapist which includes some personal acquaintance with the ache and pain of ageing as well as some of the benefits from a longer life experience. The revision has given me an opportunity to tidy up some of the clutter that came from a certain insecurity and need to impress or emulate others. I have been able to establish more of my own voice and write from an acceptance that I am who I am and no one else – something that has come with age. I have replaced three chapters which were about particular aspects of the service in which I worked and which have been superseded by change. The three new Chapters 1, 7 and 10 reflect developments in my interests and understanding about therapy with older people.

In the years between the first and second edition I returned for a while to Australia, the land of my birth, and became acquainted with the work and teaching of the Sydney psychoanalysts. This experience helped me gain a better understanding of the complex concept of projective identification which is so central to contemporary psychodynamic counselling and psychotherapy. I am especially grateful to have become acquainted with Joan Symington's developments of Esther Bick's work (1968) based on observational studies of mothers and their infants. Bick elucidated the importance of maternal holding in the early dependency relationship. Symington's work (1985) helped me understand more about problems with dependency which are revived late in life (Martindale, 1989a). I have come to see how fears of dependency and the underlying terrors are interwoven with fears of loneliness and fears of dying, and that projective identification is a major defence used to manage these fears and terrors. These ideas inform much of the new material in this book and further my aim to provide an in-depth understanding of counselling and psychotherapy with older people, as much about a way of thinking psychodynamically as about experiences of therapy with older people. I have tried to let my older clients and their carers tell their own stories to which I have added my commentary particularly about the unconscious processes.

This book aims to be inclusive of counselling and psychotherapy with older people and to reflect the overlap in training and practice of these professions. Hence the term 'therapy' is used throughout the book to refer to therapeutic work whether performed in the role of counsellor or psychotherapist. 'Psychodynamic' refers to the application of psycho-analytic ideas in various therapeutic settings. I use 'older people' to refer to those usually over 65 years of age because this is the age at which older people are eligible for the specialist 'older adult' services in which I work in the National Health Service. I am uneasy about this chronological way of allocating services and the implicit ageism, though there are undoubtedly difficulties which are particular to later life and which may worsen with age. This book describes therapy with older people who were referred by their GPs, by consultant physicians from the general hospital and rehabilitation ward, and by members of a community mental health team. For a while I was based in a long stay or continuing care service from which I describe therapeutic work with very frail and much older people and their carers. Thus, as well as giving a view of the ordinary difficulties older clients bring to therapy, this book includes some of the worst of growing old and is a testimony to the extraordinary resilience and tenacity of the human spirit.

Part I of this book concentrates on direct, face-to-face therapy with older people, whether individually, with couples or in groups. Chapter 1 introduces direct work and the theoretical concepts which underpin the book through an examination of the centrality of mourning in therapy with older people. Chapter 2 describes brief interventions in therapy with older people suffering debilitating physical illness and disability. Chapter 3 gives two detailed case studies of longer therapy addressing issues of dependency and the long term effects of trauma. Chapter 4 describes therapy with an older man who could no longer talk following a stroke. Chapter 5 describes therapy with older couples. Chapter 6 concludes Part I with an account of groups for very frail older people and their carers.

Part II of this book discusses indirect consultations in which therapeutic skills and insights are used to help those who care for older people and to train those who wish to learn to take up a therapeutic role. Chapter 7 introduces indirect consultations by studying unconscious aspects of ageist attitudes and behaviour and the importance of being able to take up a third perspective in thinking about the therapeutic couple of therapist and client, or carer and older client. Chapter 8 describes individual consultations with carers for very frail older people in long stay care and Chapter 9 gives an account of a support group for these carers. Chapter 10 concludes Part II with illustrations of teaching and learning about therapy with older people from experiences of supervising trainees.

Names and certain details have been changed to preserve confidentiality. I have used the term 'patient' to refer to older people whom I usually saw in a hospital setting because they were very ill and frail, and 'clients' to refer to older people seen in other therapeutic settings.

I have assumed that the reader may wish to dip into chapters in a different sequence from my arrangement, so each chapter is relatively self-contained. Although the first chapter gives an introduction to the main theoretical concepts, these ideas are revisited and illustrated with a wide variety of clinical material throughout the book. Readers who are unfamiliar with psychodynamic theory may find Chapter 10 a more accessible place to start because it describes experiences with trainees who were new to this way of working. Each section of the chapters begins by alerting the reader to key points about what follows, and each chapter concludes with a summary of the main themes.

As I reach the end of this revision for the new edition I am aware of what has not been possible. For example, experiences of difference and diversity such as race and sexual orientation in therapy with older people are not included because of the limitations of my experience which include the geographical and historical context in which I work. Perhaps, if I live and continue to work for another ten years and if there is a third edition... who knows? In the meantime, I hope that this second edition will inspire developments in therapy for older people and that those who write about such work will redress my omissions. I hope that the book will be of value not only to trainee and experienced therapists, but also to older people and their carers.

Paul Terry

# PART I
# DIRECT FACE TO FACE THERAPY

# 1

# To Love Life and Mourn Its End

## Introduction

The shadow of death brings an exquisite poignancy to therapy with older people. It means the therapist and older client have to manage various tensions: to appreciate the life that has been lived whilst bearing the pain about what has not been possible, the mistakes and regrets; to hold onto and savour what remains whilst being assailed by inexorable losses; to explore and pursue the developmental and creative possibilities of this last phase of life whilst knowing it is an ending, and recognising the limits imposed by one's history, constitution and ageing. In therapy these limits include the therapist's training, skills and personality, and the time that is available. In essence the tension in this work is to retain a love of life whilst mourning its end.

Mourning is central to this therapeutic work because mourning involves recognition of whom and what are valued and loved, as well as recognition of their loss. The pain evoked by loss is a reflection of our love, passion, involvement, hopes and ambitions, whether for a person, career, hobby, interest or country. The work of mourning also means acknowledging our own and others' limitations, including hatred and destructiveness, and the limits of life itself. If who and what are loved can be truly mourned then, though no longer part of our external world, they can be established in the internal world of the mind and continue to nourish and sustain our lives and our love of life. Mourning can therefore be enriching and support development and creativity in old age, as it does through all life transitions (Noonan, 1983, p. 3).

Although the theme of loss threads its way through each chapter of this book, it is important to keep in mind that the losses are reflections of the lives that have been lived, and of who and what have been cherished. Older people suffer a multitude of losses which are indicative of a multitude of experiences. They suffer loss of work and vocation because of retirement, redundancy or incapacity; and can therefore draw on histories of work, interests and hobbies, some of which they may still be able to pursue. As their bodies wear out they experience losses of physical and mental capacities, and consequent losses of independence especially when they may need others to care for them; the wrinkles, wear and tear of their bodies and minds are markers of the lives that have been lived. Children leave home. Colleagues, contemporaries, neighbours, friends, partners and pets die, and inconsolably their own children may die ahead of them. Therefore they have influenced and may continue to influence a multifarious world of interpersonal relationships, and are influenced by these relationships in their internal worlds. They face the inevitability of the ending of a long life. They have experienced, witnessed, endured and survived the joy and pain of life for a long time.

The understanding of how external losses become internal resources has come from psychoanalytic studies of mourning. The following section describes two seminal works on mourning, and introduces key theoretical concepts as they evolved in these studies and which inform much of the therapeutic work in this book.

## Two seminal psychoanalytic studies of mourning

*In Freud's study of mourning and depression he understood how unconscious hatred could obstruct mourning. Klein showed how such obstacles could be overcome through bearing painful feelings of guilt and sorrow leading to reparation and the establishment of the lost loved one in an internal world.*

Early in the history of psychoanalysis there were two outstanding studies of mourning and depression which led to the development of what is known as the Object Relations School of Thought in Psychoanalysis. Object Relations theory essentially reflects the recognition that from the beginnings of life we seek a loving relationship, and our early relationships play a critical part in our emotional development and our identity. (See Caper, 2000 for an excellent introduction to the development of Object Relations theory.) The two seminal papers were by Sigmund Freud, titled 'Mourning and Melancholia' published in 1917 and Melanie Klein's 'Mourning and its Relation to Manic-Depressive States' published in 1940. Both these papers examine the similarities and differences between mourning and depression. Freud and Klein were pioneers in the study of the unconscious, and bravely drew on their own experiences to extend the frontiers of psychological knowledge. Both papers were linked with personal grief. In Freud's case we know that he first sketched the ideas for his paper a year after the death of his father. Klein wrote her paper several years after the tragic death of her son and she even included a thinly disguised case study about her own grief in the paper. Both these seminal works were written from the heart.

Freud understood that mourning the loss of a loved one has to be worked through in minute detail; as he said 'Each single one of the memories and expectations' of the loved person has to be summoned up against reality to reach the verdict that the loved one is dead and lost forever. He described how 'extra-ordinarily' painful this process could be and puzzled over why it is so painful. Freud saw that depression, like mourning, involved an important loss but which the depressed person was unable to mourn because of strong ambivalent feelings towards the lost loved one. He recognised that in apparent self-criticisms that a depressed patient made, there were concealed criticisms against the lost one, and that these self-criticisms were in fact disguised complaints about being abandoned and left. Part of the self or ego became identified with the lost person, as Freud so memorably and poetically wrote 'the shadow of the object (the one who was lost) fell upon the ego'. Later in his work Freud realised how any loss, especially early in life, leads to important identifications that shape the ego and the nature of our character.

An illustration of Freud's insight can be seen underlying the problems presented by a man in his seventies who complained of breathing difficulties for which there was no physical basis, but which severely impaired his life over several years. He was constantly in a weak state and had to be accompanied to the assessment interview by his wife. He tended to lean on his wife because he was afraid of falling. Five years previously his eldest son died of asthma. He was very close to his son and was still tearful when speaking of him. He had become identified with his son in this debilitating physical symptom which replicated his son's asthmatic condition. In a concrete identification he unconsciously denied the loss because he felt he was his son and had not lost him. He was unable to mourn and had become depressed. The shadow of his son had fallen on his ego.

In 'Mourning and its Relation to Manic-Depressive States' Klein agreed with Freud that the central tasks in mourning are to face the reality of the loss in the external world and establish the loved one internally. Klein discovered that, in the unconscious, experiences of bereavement revive our earliest experiences of loss first encountered in infancy in relation to the mother or primary caretaker. Furthermore, Klein developed an understanding of how in infancy and childhood the experience of loss leads to identifying with and internalising important figures like our parents and family, with the result that the child builds up an internal world which is peopled with all these figures. Klein's work thus sheds further light on how in mourning the task of establishing the loved one internally is accomplished. Klein also went some way in explaining why mourning is so very painful and may endure for a long time. Following bereavement it is as though all the loved figures in the internal world are lost, and the internal world is in a state of devastation.

## Mourning in infancy

It may seem strange in an introduction to therapy in later life to turn to infancy, but psychoanalytic and psychodynamic therapy is informed by an understanding of how early experiences of infancy and childhood crucially influence development of the personality and personal relationships. In particular the internalisation of early life experiences and relationships creates an unconscious internal world of 'object relations' which influences and is influenced by experiences and relationships throughout life. Later influences may include the experience of therapy, so understanding more about the internalisation contributes to insight into the therapeutic process. Infancy has particular relevance for therapy with older people because ageing often brings the need to be dependent again on the care of others and thus revives, consciously and unconsciously, our earliest experience of dependency and being in a dependent relationship. (Fears of dependency which are revived in later life are discussed in Chapter 7.)

The following is a sketch of Klein's understanding of how the internal world is first established, and of the nature of infantile states of mind that are revived in later experiences of bereavement. Klein emphasised that for the infant or small child with little or no sense of time or continuity, a temporary absence of the mother, as well as major losses experienced such as in weaning, can be experienced as irrevocable losses, equivalent in important respects to an adult's experience of loss and bereavement. So for the infant and child, when faced with an absence that may feel eternal, there is the mourner's task of needing to establish the lost loved one internally in the mind. Klein saw too that just as for adults, experiences of loss and frustration for the infant and child stir powerful conflicting feelings between love and hate for the one who is missed.

Klein introduced the concept of unconscious phantasy to describe what she understood about the infant's, child's and adult's unconscious experience. Klein traced different phantasies and anxieties which were linked to how external figures are established in the internal world, to the infant's and child's capacities and to the love and care they receive. Klein proposed that just as the infant takes in food and nourishment so in unconscious phantasy the infant internalises experiences of nurture and security of mother's care; and just as the infant expels waste products such as faeces and urine so in unconscious phantasy the infant projects unpleasant emotional experiences into the external world. The fragmented and unintegrated state of the infant's physical and psychological capacities mean that at first what is internalised is also fragmented, such as isolated aspects of mother's care, like the sound of mother's voice, or her cradling arms, rather than an identification with mother as a whole person. It is the mother or primary caretaker who by physically and mentally holding the infant gives the infant an experience of continuity and coherence, essentially by *holding* all the different fragments of the infant's experience in her mind (Bick, 1968). For example the mother helps the infant to know that the infant, who was crying at one moment, is the same infant who smiles at the next. Gradually the infant becomes able to recognise a sense of continuity and wholeness in his or her own identity and recognise the mother as a whole person.

From the start of life there is a complex interaction between the internal and external world, especially between the ambivalence of loving and hating feelings and good and bad experiences. The infant does not have the capacity to manage the conjunction of opposite feelings and experiences, and at first needs to keep them as separate as possible, out of fear that the bad will spoil the good. Thus the infant *splits* feelings and experiences into either good or bad, and is inclined to exaggerate the differences, idealising the good as a necessary source of strength and inner security against the bad. Moreover, these very opposite feelings are projected into what becomes polarised loved or hated external figures who are then established as such figures in the internal world. Klein described this state of mind and the accompanying anxieties and defences as the *'paranoid-schizoid position'*, indicating that it is a state of mind to which we can return throughout life especially when under conditions of extreme stress.

Klein's child patients sometimes revealed harsh and cruel internal parental figures in contrast to their actual parents. Klein soon appreciated that as a result of projection of feelings there was not a direct correspondence between the external figures in reality and how they were internalised which she described as *'internal objects'*. She thus developed Freud's understanding of projective processes into the concept of *projective identification* in which in unconscious phantasy parts of the self are split off and denied and projected into the other who is then identified with those aspects of the self (Klein, 1946). Projective identification has been widely recognised as perhaps Klein's most influential contribution to psychoanalytic understanding and has had far-reaching consequences in contemporary psychoanalytic schools of thought. Although projective identification refers to an unconscious phantasy, Klein's followers have discovered that it can actually have an effect on the recipient of the projection who through subtle influences of verbal and non-verbal behaviour, can come to actually feel what is projected into them. This discovery led to understanding more about the crucial role of the mother or primary carer.

Wilfrid Bion, one of Klein's most influential protégés, described the mother's capacity to *contain* the infant's projected emotional states as an essential contribution to the infant's development (Bion, 1962). So, by virtue of her capacity to hold together the fragments of the infant's experience, as well as her receptiveness to the infant's emotional states, particularly being able to take in his or her distress and transform it with love and understanding, the mother eventually enables the infant, then child, to bear difficult feelings. Thus along with the infant's developing physical and cognitive capacities, there is less splitting, less need to project, and a growing sense of being more emotionally integrated, whole and able to relate to whole people. Consequently the internal world becomes inhabited with whole figures.

However, these developments towards integration usher in new *depressive anxieties* which come from the realisation that the nurturing mother is the same mother who is sometimes absent, a mother who is both loved and hated, and that the self who loves is also the self who hates. Thus the experience of loss of the whole mother presents the infant or child with much pain, because in phantasy the mother is felt to be irretrievably lost and the infant or child feels responsible for the loss because of hatred and aggression. The infant or child is therefore faced with painful feelings of guilt and sorrow, pining for the lost mother and for him- or herself who has lost the mother. These are at first very difficult feelings for the infant or child to manage without recourse to the early defences of splitting, denial and projective identification and what Klein described as *manic defences* which are characterised by control, contempt and triumph. However with repeated experiences of mother's love and care, and with developing emotional resources there develops a capacity to bear the tragedy of the loss, guilt and sorrow which leads to reparation, a desire to make good the damage and the establishment of the lost loved one internally.

Although Klein emphasised unconscious phantasy and the internal world, she also understood the importance of external reality in establishing the loved one internally. It is the reality of the presence of the mother or primary carer, her reliability and consistency, and most of all her love that assuages the infant's and child's fears and worst phantasies stirred by her absences. The mother's loving presence brings hope in the face of devastation and ultimately enables a sense of duration and permanence in the internal world (Likierman, 2001), so that, as Freud understood, eventually as an adult mourning we can face the reality of loss of our loved ones and our own death. However, in order for this to be achieved the absences and losses in infancy and childhood have to be overcome by working through again and again the suffering and need for reparation, in order to restore and reestablish our loved ones in the internal world.

## Adult mourning

The appreciation of infant experiences of mourning is especially important because these states of mind are revived in adult experiences of loss and grief. Following a bereavement the internal world is in a state of devastation, not only the loved one is felt to be lost but all the loved and loving internal figures, particularly important early primary figures like mother and father, are felt to be lost as well. The self can then feel at the mercy of hated and hating internal figures which may lead to frightening or even persecutory internal states. Thus the bereaved may feel in pieces, in a fragmented state and unable to manage other than by extremely polarised and split feelings, making a sharp divide between loving and hating feelings.

A woman was brought into hospital in a weak and malnourished condition, convinced her neighbours were plotting to have her evicted from her home. She had worked conscientiously in a commercial business that was like an extended family to her. She was devoted to her work, it was the centre of her world, and when she retired a few years previously she came to feel that she had lost everything. She then believed that anything good she had left would be taken away from her.

Klein understood that the mourner's task is 'with anguish' to rebuild the internal world, to reinstate the lost loved ones. In the unconscious the mourner feels responsible for the death and destruction, helpless to repair or restore the lost one, terrified he or she will not survive without the loved one and at the same time feels guilt and remorse about anger towards the loved one out of frustration about their limitations. If the mourner has the capacity to bear the guilt, responsibility and sorrow, then these feelings can fuel the repair and restoration of the loved one in the internal world.

An 83 year-old woman, Mrs Ames, was referred to me because she was having panic attacks, especially at night. She was soon to be admitted to residential accommodation because she had become too frail to live on her own. Mrs Ames told me that her husband had died four years ago. She said she was very attached to him. He was a carpenter and built most of the furniture in their house. She awoke one night to find him dead alongside her in bed. She thought 'Whatever has become of him!' She feared she might die too. Mrs Ames said she was the last surviving member of her family. Her father had died also 'quite suddenly', when she was just a girl still at school. The family were then threatened with being put in a home. I said I thought in her panic attacks she relived her husband's death and was in a panic that she would die in the night too; she was still grieving a much loved husband. She responded by saying how helpful her husband had been, he used to help her in the kitchen. She showed me a photograph of them both, a handsome couple. She said she could see that she had been ill since his death. Finally, she talked about going to the care home. She had visited it and liked the idea of being there. It was near a weekly club she attended, so she would be able to keep going to the club.

Mrs Ames was engaged in mourning again the many losses in her life. Her associations to her panics revealed the earlier losses which were revived by the imminent loss of her home: the death of her husband whom she was still grieving and the similarly sudden death of her father. She was thus bringing to the surface her infantile anxieties, showing me how this old woman was reminded of her father's death when she was just a girl and of the threat of being put in a home, which was now really going to happen. Showing me the photograph gave me a glimpse of her internal world and the happy couple she had inside her despite her external losses. This internal security helped her face the loss of her home and make the best of the move to the care home, keeping some links with her recent interests through her club.

## Projective identification and mourning

*Further psychoanalytic work has amplified the understanding of projective identification as a defence which obstructs mourning. The use of this defence is connected with the fears of one's own death triggered in bereavement.*

Projective identification has various uses. It can be used to communicate emotional states, as described previously in mother and infant relationships whereby the mother gets to know her infant and then helps him or her to understand him- or herself. It continues throughout life to be an important means of communication, particularly for unconscious states of mind that we may find unbearable. In intimate relationships we may unconsciously lodge certain unmanageable aspects of ourselves in the other person with the hope that we may eventually retrieve these qualities and feel more integrated, as discussed in Chapter 5 about therapy with couples. It can also be used aggressively to possess and control and deny separateness.

The mourner needs to be able to tolerate separateness. Part of the unconscious hatred of the loved one comes from a fear of separateness and wanting to remain merged with the loved one. Freud observed that his very self-critical depressed patient had made a concrete identification with the lost loved one, effectively treating part of his own ego as the loved one against whom he harboured unconscious criticisms. It is then as though the loved one is possessed by the self and no longer lost. Anger with the loved one is denied by displacing the anger onto oneself. However, the anger is expressed indirectly by possessing and controlling the loved one in one's mind, not allowing him or her to die or be separate. We now understand the underlying process as projective identification being used to deny separateness by treating the other person as an extension of oneself.

The post-Kleinian developments of projective identification are therefore very useful in understanding more about the work of mourning and particularly the manic defences which, if they become entrenched, impede the work of mourning. An illustration of this projective process can be seen in a therapist who was feeling very guilty about his work with a woman. He felt he wasn't giving his client enough help or giving her enough time. The client kept complaining about her husband who had left her with a small child. However, apparently this woman had for some years been unable to look after the child herself. In the *transference* the client was treating the therapist as if he was her husband and had transferred unconscious feelings about her neglectful husband onto the therapist. In terms of the underlying projective process the internal figure of her husband in her mind contained her feelings about her own neglect of her children. In the transference she thus projected her feelings of guilt and neglect into her therapist who became identified with these feelings. In the *counter-transference* (meaning all the feelings experienced by the therapist) the therapist began to feel some of his client's projected feelings about neglect and guilt

11

which he mistakenly identified as his own. In so far as the client tended to dominate the therapist's thoughts she also began to exert some control over him.

The client complained that she couldn't stop thinking about her husband. She said she even thought about him in the shower. So, although she was tormented by this preoccupation, in a sense it meant that her husband was still very much with her and in this way she denied the loss which contributed to her difficulty in working through the grief. Moreover, in her internal world the figure of her husband was possessed and controlled by the projection into him of this neglectful aspect of herself. Her husband may well have been neglectful too, just as her therapist may have had reasons to feel guilty, but it is in the nature of this projective defence that it often finds realistic hooks for the projections. The therapist therefore needs to engage in a careful process of self-monitoring to tease out what may be projected by the client and what may belong to the therapist. Projective identification does not always mean that feelings are evoked in the therapist. There may be times when the therapist understands the unconscious phantasy of what he or she is meant to feel without being affected by those feelings.

The detailed understanding of this projective process helps further illuminate the establishment or reestablishment of loved ones in the internal world following bereavement. If there is a capacity to mourn and bear separateness, then there is a desire to restore the loved one in the mind out of love, not from a wish to possess and control. The projections will be withdrawn out of concern for the loved one. The mourner is thus able to allow the loved one to die and to install the loved one in a symbolical way in the mind. On the other hand in a frightened state of mind the bereaved person will be more likely to resort to projective identification to hold onto the loved one at all costs. The loved one may then be internalised in a concrete way that possesses and controls, and may be tormenting.

## Fear of death

The fear of separateness and the use of projective identification to possess and control triggered by the bereavement of a loved one is associated with a fear for one's own survival following the sense of the devastation of the internal world in which all the loved ones are felt to be lost. The resulting concrete identification may then be an early response to bereavement which if it persists will obstruct mourning (Steiner, 1993). Paradoxically, in the resort to this use of projective identification the fear of dying oneself is of course compounded by concretely identifying with the lost dead person. At its most extreme this form of identification can be seen in very severely depressed people who become mute, comatose and who would surely die if it were not for external intervention. A less extreme example can be seen in the following:

Mrs Foley, a woman in her early seventies, was admitted to hospital in a suicidal state. Her suicidal thoughts developed following the deteriorating physical condition of her husband who was ten years her senior. He was losing his mobility, becoming more and more dependent on her and feeling more and more hopeless about his physical state. Although Mrs Foley was herself physically fit, she became unable to leave the house on her own. She spent most of the time sitting with her husband, her arms folded in a worried state. Her recurring thoughts were of hanging herself and she associated these thoughts with stories of public hangings when she was a child. She acknowledged a sense of tragedy about her husband whom she loved but said she was unable to cry. She kept saying how very guilty she felt about her suicidal thoughts and about being in hospital. She also expressed guilt about an incident in her life many years earlier. When I tried to explore the nature of her suicidal thoughts she reproached me saying I was forcing these thoughts into her mind, whereas she didn't want to think about them. I felt very uncomfortable. With hindsight I can see she was giving me a taste of her experience of what it was like to feel helpless and guilty.

I think Mrs Foley found difficulty mourning the losses following her husband's severe physical decline, including the anticipation of his death. She became quite identified with him, immobilised and unable to do anything on her own. She expressed anger against herself in thoughts of hanging herself, as though like others she had observed in the public executions, she had committed a crime for which she must be punished. I think her unconscious crime was her anger and frustration with her husband who became disabled and might soon die and leave her. The identification with him kept him inside her, and at the same time indirectly expressed some of her anger towards him, for example by becoming something of an invalid herself and being unable to look after him. Her suicidal preoccupations may also have been a way of trying to manage her own fears of death, which were stirred by the anticipation of the loss of her husband. These fears were unconsciously communicated to others who feared for her life, admitted her to hospital and kept a close eye on her.

Another illustration of difficulties in mourning is Mr Powell, a 70 year-old man who, when he suffered a second stroke, had to be admitted into long stay care because his wife could no longer look after him at home. Previously a pleasant natured and popular man, once in long stay he began punching staff and was often verbally abusive to them. He masturbated in public and made sexually provocative remarks to the female staff, admitting to taking pleasure in 'winding' them up. Over and over again he would insist on being taken to the toilet when he had no need of it.

Mr Powell could not bear his grief and sorrow about the dreadful consequences of his stroke. Instead he made the care staff feel his sense of outrage, disgust and helplessness by his aggressive and controlling behaviour. Mr Powell's strokes were undoubtedly a brush with death. Most of all he was unable to mourn the end of his own life.

Hanna Segal (1986) has written about psychoanalytic work with an elderly man which focussed on this man's unconscious fear of death. He was in treatment for 18 months which finished when he was 75. He led a healthy and vigorous life for another 11 years. Segal described events during the last evening of this man's life. The events were reported to her by the man's son. It seems this man had a long conversation with his wife during which he was concerned to establish the exact whereabouts of his family. Though his wife had told him before, he said 'it had never seemed real'. This time he said 'I know they are there and it is quite real to me'. Segal understands these events as part of this man preparing for his death by placing his family in reality, relinquishing of omnipotent control and allowing them to live on without him; and placing them in his internal world 'without coercion or control'. (p. 181)

Karina Codeco Barone described some therapeutic work with a five year-old girl who was suffering from a life threatening tumour (2005). In hospital the girl was forlorn and lifeless. When she was helped to play the girl soon portrayed scenarios in which a girl doll was going to die and nothing could be done to save her. The meaning of the child's play was not interpreted, but over some time the play changed. The girl introduced a story which she repeated and in which she encouraged her therapist to join her celebrating the girl doll's birthday. This is a touching example of how experiences of being able have someone take in and digest fears of death can lead to hope.

In *Making Death Thinkable* the author Franco De Masi (2004) maintains that our own death is essentially unthinkable. He points out that when we think of our death it is often from the perspective implicitly of still being present, for example of looking on at our own funeral.

Unconsciously too, however painful or tormenting death may be portrayed in dreams, the dreamer is usually present. What is unimaginable is nothingness. De Masi describes our death as an excessive trauma for our mind, he says:

> 'our death as individuals is an experience of separation unlike any other form of mourning, and therefore it triggers a specific anxiety which cannot be worked through easily or assimilated to other partings.' (p. 112)

De Masi concludes that 'Reparation can only be achieved *through the past*, through the projection of our past into the future, *in the future of others*' (author's italics). But he adds 'The real tragedy, unthinkable and beyond every possible reparation, is not so much the death of any one individual self, but the destruction of humanity and the universe which has given us a home and allows us to experience a sense of continuity; the irreparable damage is the total destruction of the world and its future memory.' (p. 124)

De Masi helps us understand why anticipation of one's own death may have become particularly terrifying since the development and amassing of enough nuclear weapons to destroy our entire civilisation. As Robert Hinshelwood (2002) has written:

> 'We each have methods of coping with a desire for immortality, by means of institutionalised religion, family descendants or physical or academic achievements. But (in a nuclear war) none of these will remain, so unlike death in ordinary war, we know there will be no-one left to glorify the war and the sacrifice or to keep us and our achievements in their hearts.' (p. 253)

Elliot Jaques (1965) has written of how the awareness of death precipitates a mid-life crisis. He has examined the effects of this awareness in the differences between creativity in early and in later life. He describes how achieving an acceptance of hatred, destructiveness and the inevitability of death lead to a mature creativity which reflects a 'constructive resignation to the imperfections of men and to shortcomings in one's own work'. This constructive resignation 'then imparts serenity to life and work' (p. 232). Thus being able to mourn in old age, which means accepting the inevitability of death and acknowledging hatred and human destructiveness, can bring a serenity to our final years.

# Summary

Mourning is central to therapeutic work with older people because it recognises in loss the loves, passions, achievements and attachments in life. In the internal world mourning establishes who and what have been loved and lost externally, in a way that they may continue to sustain and nourish one's life. Psychoanalytic studies of grief and bereavement provide an insight into the mourning process and why it is so very painful and may endure for a long time. Each loss revives earlier ones and our unconscious internal world is felt to be bereft of all the loved and loving internal figures. Unconscious hatred, fears of separateness and fears of death create particular obstacles and can lead to depression and a denial of loss in a concrete identification with the lost loved person through the use of projective identification. Mourning means coming to accept the limitations of our loved one and life itself. Reestablishing the lost one internally comes through reparation from bearing hatred, aggression, destructiveness, guilt and sorrow. It also means bearing separateness, retrieving projected aspects of the self that are used to possess and control, and thus being able to establish the loved one internally in a symbolical way that recognises loss.

In therapy to enable mourning means providing the kind of holding and containment the mother provides for her infant. Just as the mother's reliable and consistent presence helps the infant accommodate early experiences of absence and loss, so the therapist's maintaining a reliable and consistent therapeutic frame helps the mourning process. Within the security of the therapeutic frame the therapist offers receptiveness for the bereaved's unmanageable feelings. It is particularly the therapist's capacity to bear what is most unbearable, unconscious and projected, and gradually help the client retrieve these projections that enables the client to work through the grieving process. In many respects these elements of mourning are central to the aims of psychodynamic therapy to help the client regain lost projected parts of him- or herself. These aims are manifest in the work of addressing the transference and counter-transference, and the underlying projective processes by which a client is depleted of emotional resources (Steiner, 1989).

The challenge for the therapist is to remain receptive to the projections which can mean that the client unconsciously may mobilise the therapist's own fears, and perhaps most difficult the fear of death, which in our contemporary society has become especially terrifying because of the nuclear threat to civilisation. Crucial elements in the therapeutic work will be absences, breaks, and the ending of the therapeutic relationship, because each loss of the therapist is an opportunity to address the very difficulties of grieving and letting go for which the client is in need of help.

If we can help our older clients mourn then they may be less depleted by projective processes and thus have a more complete and integrated sense of themselves. They may gain enrichment from an internal sense of what has disappeared externally, and be strengthened to pursue creative possibilities of later life. At the very least they may achieve serenity in this last phase of life.

# 2

# BRIEF INTERVENTIONS

## Introduction

This chapter is about brief therapy in relation to grief and bereavement following illness and disability. These older clients were not regarded as psychiatrically ill and were referred from a rehabilitation ward. My contact with them was short, sometimes only one or two meetings because they were discharged home or transferred into residential accommodation. However these brief interventions were often sufficient to facilitate or support a mourning process. I hope this material will provide an opportunity to study what can usefully be offered by way of therapy in brief contacts with older people and their carers. I hope too it will be an opportunity to think about some of the difficulties. The work illustrates a technique for brief work which involves thinking about, but not interpreting, transferences and unconscious phantasies stirred in these patients' and carers' internal worlds by physical illness. The transferences were usually not interpreted because it would have been unhelpful to encourage a dependency relationship in view of the brevity of the contact. The work shows how carers can help their older clients by giving them some time to talk about their feelings and by the carers reflecting on their own emotional reactions as a means of understanding their clients. A wide-ranging account of other forms of brief psychodynamic therapy with older people is discussed by Sian Critchley-Robbins (2004).

## Illness, disability and bereavement

*My response to an early referral reveals what can be overlooked because of eagerness to start seeing clients. Subsequent examples illustrate how providing time and space for these clients' feelings quickly led to the unfolding of bereavement in response to illness and disability.*

## An early referral

Soon after taking up a post working with older people, following a visit to the acute ward of a general hospital I was asked to see an elderly man who was soon to be transferred to the rehabilitation ward. His doctor was worried about this man's depressed mood since a recent hospitalisation for a physical illness. I was pleased to be referred someone and to be commencing some 'real' work, after having spent several days talking to various members of staff, attending ward rounds and other meetings. I was to see the patient in his single room. His doctor took me in and introduced me. I found a small thin man sitting stiffly in an armchair by his bed. He was fully dressed in a grey suit and looked displeased. The doctor left us. I pulled up another chair, sat down and asked him how he felt about talking with me. He replied straight way that he did not want to see me and he had nothing to say! I think I stayed rather longer and tried to persuade him more than I should have because of my keenness to get on with some client work. But he remained adamant in his refusal to talk. Eventually I left, very disappointed.

## Mr Miller – whose upset was in his house

Mr Miller, a 76 year-old man was referred to me because the staff were concerned that Mr Miller's physical condition had deteriorated very quickly since his admission to the rehabilitation ward a few weeks earlier. He was now unable to walk and would be confined to a wheelchair for the rest of his life. He lived with his wife in a small two storey house. The staff felt he could not accept that he would no longer be able to go upstairs. He was worried about how his wife would cope and that he would be 'totally marooned'.

The ward sister asked me if I would see Mr Miller in a small side room alongside the nurses' office. This was a narrow room with a single bed and locker. There was just enough space to fit a couple of chairs. When Mr Miller was wheeled in, he towered over me, a large man with swollen legs and bandages showing from under his trouser cuffs. He had a sad expression. I asked him how he felt about seeing me. He seemed pleased. He said he was grateful to have this opportunity to talk to someone.

Mr Miller spoke about his house being 'upset' because they had to get rid of two armchairs in the living room on the ground floor to make way for a bed to be brought down for him. I said that I thought *he* was probably upset. He almost laughed in agreement saying he supposed they were all upset, especially his wife. Later, he said how he would be lost if it weren't for his wife and he wept. When he had recovered his composure, he went on to say that the physiotherapists said they wouldn't take any responsibility for him if he went upstairs, but he thought he was fit enough. Then he talked about going to see his doctor just a few weeks ago, when he was immediately put into hospital. I felt the force of his shock as he said this. I said he had suffered an awful blow and I thought he was still shocked by what had happened. He heaved a sigh of relief and agreed, saying the doctor said he was in a 'terrible state'. I had the impression Mr Miller had not appreciated how ill he had become. He was shocked to be suddenly admitted to hospital.

He looked sad again and said if only he had gone to the doctor 12 months earlier, perhaps he would still be able to climb the stairs. He then described his house in more detail. There were just two rooms on the ground floor, a hall and steps into the garden. He seemed forlorn at the thought of not being able to go into his garden again. I felt upset and asked about the possibility of ramps for the steps so he could go out. He didn't feel confident he and his wife could manage with ramps.

The only bathroom was on the first floor. They had been given a commode but he worried about managing without a bathroom. He talked about getting a stair lift installed, but then said he thought it would take too long. I wondered, to myself, whether he feared he might not live much longer. He asked me if he would be going to the day hospital once he was discharged from the rehabilitation ward. I assured him I understood it was arranged for him. He then asked if the further tests and scan he had, meant that he would be cured? I felt very uncomfortable and said 'we don't know', but that I thought he wanted me to understand he hoped he could get better. He agreed about the hope though he then looked sad. He said his wife was coming tomorrow. I asked if he would like me to see him with his wife. He was pleased at this suggestion. I concluded the meeting and made arrangements to see them the following week.

The next week, John, the nurse who was Mr Miller's keyworker (his designated nurse), was on duty. John told me that Mr Miller was sometimes able to do things for himself, like shaving, but at other times was unable to do those same things, especially when he was miserable. I asked John, provided Mr and Mrs Miller agreed, if he would attend my next meeting with them. I explained that I thought it would help him to have a better understanding of Mr and Mrs Miller's feelings. John appeared somewhat bemused but was agreeable. The couple also agreed. We all met in the side room, almost sitting in each other's laps.

Mrs Miller was well-groomed, smartly dressed and looked a little younger than her husband. She smiled and said that her sister had recently joked with her, saying 'You married him for better or for worse'. Together Mr and Mrs Miller said 'and this is the worse'. I felt moved in the presence of a loving relationship. I said Mr Miller was very appreciative of his wife. He talked about how important she was to him and cried. Mrs Miller showed great sympathy for her husband, talking about how difficult she knew it was for someone like him who had been 'so independent' now to be so very dependent. With a sense of resignation she said 'We'll doubtless bark at one another' and added it would be important not to 'bottle things up'. Soon after I drew the meeting to a close. They were both grateful and felt they would not need to see me again. I invited them to contact me if they wished. Mr Miller was to be discharged in the next few days. This meeting finished after half an hour. It was shorter than the previous one with Mr Miller on his own, which had been for an hour.

## Commentary

Looking back at the early referral I feel somewhat embarrassed at my eagerness to begin seeing clients because of the way it devalued the importance of thinking about the organisational setting and spending time gathering information to assess how best to work within it. Yet, some time later, when a trainee clinical psychologist joined me on a placement in the hospital, I was indignant that he seemed to feel the real work had only started the day he saw his first patient. I felt he had dismissed the importance of the other activities, like staff and ward meetings to which he had been introduced. This kind of patient-oriented view of the work to which I and my trainee were drawn, can obstruct thinking about the nature of the referral, about who or what is the underlying problem, as distinct from who or what is presented as the problem. In that first referral on the acute ward, it may have been more helpful to have spent some time with the staff talking about their concern about the 'depressed' patient. Why was it necessary to call in an expert? What might the referral have been communicating about the staff's feelings? What could it mean to this man to have me brought in, to be confronted with 'a shrink?' He may have thought they felt he was going mad.

By the time I saw Mr Miller I had decided that it would be better to try to involve patients' keyworkers. I describe consultations with key-workers in Chapter 8. Although I felt pleased with the meetings with Mr Miller, I remained disappointed and puzzled by his keyworker's apparent incomprehension when I suggested he attend the meeting with Mr and Mrs Miller. On the one hand John seemed to have noticed how Mr Miller's misery affected his ability to do things for himself, but on the other hand John showed little interest in being involved at the meeting or in later discussions with me. It was as if Mr Miller's misery was handed over to me in the referral. Then John and perhaps the other staff could remain distant from the grief. Thus my role could be used by the hospital as a way of avoiding thinking about the patients' emotional distress. My invitation to John was a challenge to this organisational defence, but it failed.

Looking in detail at the material I am struck that by providing Mr Miller with a space in which he could talk and I could listen and think about his experience, he quickly brought a picture of the 'upset house' and difficult adjustments which were being made to accommodate his disability. I think he was also telling me about his internal world in which he was trying to accommodate his emotional upset, though consciously he located the upset in his house. He laughed with relief when his upset could be acknowledged. This moment of feeling held in my mind enabled him to acknowledge his helplessness and dependency. He tried to restore his equilibrium by denying his disability, but then was in touch with his shock at being admitted to hospital. When I could register and articulate the shock, he could acknowledge his 'terrible state' through the words of his doctor. He was then confronted with the sorrowful thought that if he hadn't denied the state of his illness for so long, he might have been treated successfully. It may be that this thought in which he assumed some responsibility for the damaging effects of his illness, protected him from more pain of seeing that nothing could have been done to prevent or cure his affliction. However, I think it is a reflection, unconsciously, of an internal world which is in a terrible state because he feels his destructive feelings have got the upper hand. I was affected by his upset and started to think about how he might organise some ramps, as if he had no internal resources with which to think. Perhaps I tried to provide a ramp for myself over uncomfortable feelings. I can now see it was difficult for me to stay with his despair that nothing more could be done for his physical condition, time was running out and perhaps he would soon die. Though wondering about his anticipation of death, I was unable to speak about it. Perhaps sensing my reluctance to speak about his fears of death he turned to me as a medical authority who would join in a denial of such fears by reassuring him he would be cured. I took shelter behind a collective 'we' who did not know.

As far as I understood a recovery was unlikely, but my understanding of the medical condition was paltry and in retrospect it would have been better to say that, and provide some space for his fears by suggesting perhaps he was afraid he would not recover. Sometimes I found it difficult to grasp the details of the patients' medical conditions. Instead, I felt impelled to think about the possible emotional meaning of the patients' illnesses, in contrast to the rest of the staff who were more often preoccupied with the physical state and seemed reluctant to take in the clients' feelings. I thus perpetuated an unfortunate split in which I remained an 'expert' about the clients' emotions but relatively ignorant of their physical illnesses.

Mr Miller's references to his wife seemed a cue that he wanted to include her in the counselling sessions. The second meeting was important in supporting the marital relationship to manage what they described as the 'for worse' in their marital vows. The marital relationship finds echoes in an internal world, where the primary figures include a couple, probably a parental couple, working together to manage loving and destructive feelings. It was helpful to acknowledge Mr Miller's love and gratitude for his wife, to support the external relationship and to recognise the strength of his loving feelings, when internally he felt so damaged by destructiveness. This intervention also supported his wife, evident when she could anticipate that their anger and frustration would need to be expressed in 'barking' at one another. I do not want to suggest an idealised 'Darby and Joan' view of older couples (later material in Chapter 5 soon dispels any such view) nor do I wish to suggest that only couple relationships offer such support. I simply want to draw attention to the importance of including family and carers in the counselling, and of supporting loving relationships.

## Further illustrations of bereavement reactions to illness and disability

*In these bereavement reactions shock, denial and sadness were more readily expressed than anger and guilt. Anger and guilt were usually expressed indirectly. Family members may also be grieving the patient's illness.*

### Mr Sewell – who used humour to manage his grief

The experience of shock is a recurring theme. Another man, Mr Sewell, also in his seventies, whom I saw once weekly for six weeks, told me again and again of the circumstances of the stroke which suddenly brought him into hospital. He had been on holiday with his wife in a hotel in Spain. They were very happy celebrating his retirement. It was like a second honeymoon. He collapsed in the bedroom as they were preparing to go down for dinner, his wife ran for help. The stroke left him paralysed on the right side of his body. At times his speech was a bit slurred and sometimes saliva dribbled from his mouth. During the first two meetings he wept profusely and with obvious relief.

At the third meeting, on Mr Sewell's instigation, his wife and son joined us. Mrs Sewell was a glamorous woman, probably also in her seventies, with a blonde coiffure and wearing a white trouser suit. Mr Sewell mentioned his crying in the previous meetings, making a joke about staining the carpet in my room with his tears. He described himself as a 'sad clown'. I said I thought he was brokenhearted. He cried again. Later his wife cried too. However, she and her son, who arrived late, were uncomfortable when Mr Sewell wept and they encouraged him to make his usual jokes. After a while he talked about his plans to buy a smaller bungalow which would be more manageable and designed for his disability. But, he wondered, what if he had another stroke, 'it would all be in vain'. I said I felt he was worrying about having another stroke and dying and concerned about his wife who would be left.

At the next meeting Mr Sewell was on his own. He was able to talk about some of the difficulty he experienced in coming to terms with the implications of his stroke. He had made some recovery and could walk a little with the assistance of the physiotherapist. He kept asking the staff on the ward how much more recovery he could expect, but he was aware that he was inclined 'to give myself the answer I want'. He imagined his paralysed arm recovering and being able to drive again. At the same time he was trying to make plans for the future which took his disability into account. He was worried that his feelings were 'self pity'. I talked to him about his sorrow which was part of adjusting to the future.

Before the fifth meeting I was asked to contact Mr Sewell's son on his mobile phone. He told me that Mrs Sewell had been diagnosed with cancer and would soon have to undergo an operation. He and his mother wanted to keep this secret from Mr Sewell for fear of upsetting him. I encouraged them to be open with Mr Sewell. Mrs Sewell came to the next meeting where Mr Sewell spoke tearfully about his wife's cancer and his fears for her. I said this was another shock when they had not recovered from the shock of his stroke. At the end of this painful meeting, Mrs Sewell stopped in the doorway and asked me how I managed all this sadness. I felt a bit thrown by this question. She didn't come to the final meeting. Mr Sewell explained she had problems with the car, 'three punctures'. He talked about his worries about her cancer and the operation and whether she would survive. He was to go to a nursing home while his wife was in hospital. What was hardest for Mr Sewell was not knowing what would happen.

## Commentary

An important aspect of the therapist's role in these meetings is to be able to absorb the shock of a disabling illness, much like the shock of bereavement. Joan Bicknell (1983) has given a detailed description of the bereavement she saw in families with a handicapped child. Foremost is the reaction of *shock*, followed by *panic*, *denial* and *grief* which includes *anger* and *guilt*, before there can be any acceptance of the tragedy. For these older people there is a grieving for their former able-bodied selves. The parallels with bereavement are close because such illnesses can be a forewarning of death, with a chilling reality: it is not uncommon for stroke patients to suffer multiple strokes and die from them, or for older people to die soon after an admission to hospital. It is important for therapist and carers to be able to face the reality of the patients' fears of death and particularly for the therapist to be alert to conscious and unconscious allusions to death. The difficulty for the therapist or carer is that the older client's fears of death stir up one's own infantile terror of a parent dying, as well as one's own fear of dying. For the elderly couple there is also the worry about who will die first. My impression was that Mr Sewell worried about his wife being left on her own, and when she was diagnosed with cancer he then faced being left without her.

Whether to say or do something which will be upsetting to an older person who is in a vulnerable state is a frequent question. More often than not, family or carers confuse their own upset with the patient's and may project their upset into the patient; so it is not clear in the wish to prevent upset, whether they are protecting the patient or themselves. There is too a question of whether older people having survived a lifetime of experiences, need this kind of protection. Certainly, I would not have agreed to be party to concealing information from Mr Sewell because of the dishonesty it would introduce into the therapeutic relationship and because it would have implied I thought he couldn't take it and projected vulnerability into him.

Several times Mr Sewell talked about his worries about his wife handling the car on her own, which was a way he expressed worries about his wife managing without him. The image of the punctured tyres vividly conveyed fears about her state. Of course he was also worried about her managing practicalities like the car, but it is useful to keep in mind both the external circumstances and the internal states they convey. Unlike Mrs Miller discussed previously, who was able to support her husband, Mrs Sewell was in no state to bear her husband's anxieties, because her emotional capacities had been punctured by her own traumatic diagnosis. With hindsight I think her question to me as she left the room, asking about how I managed the distress, was asking me how she was going to manage it. This kind of question, or Mr Miller telling me at the end of the first meeting that his wife was visiting, are examples of what is sometimes known as a *doorknob communication*, because of the recognition that apparently throwaway remarks, when arriving or leaving a therapy session, nearly always carry an important message.

Mr Sewell used humour to try to manage his grief. A sense of humour is a useful way of coping, of getting through otherwise intolerable difficulties, but like all defences, when resorted to excessively, it can create further problems. Dorothy Judd (1989) in her book about working with a dying child, reports research which showed that families, friends and carers of patients with cancer believed they have to remain 'cheerful, positive and optimistic' in their relationships with the patients. She notes how keeping the hospital atmosphere as 'jolly as possible' may be used unconsciously to suppress angry reactions from the patients and to 'lift' the patients out of their depression. This jollity can create a deeper despair if the patients feel that no one can bear their sad or angry feelings.

Mr Sewell shows how patients can collude in maintaining a jolly atmosphere. When he brought humour to the therapy sometimes it prevented him from being in touch with his grief and therefore obstructed working through the bereavement connected with his illness. When I did not join in on the jokes and tried to think about the humour, there was more space for his grief which led to some movement towards accepting the reality of his losses.

### Mrs Hill – who could only hear her daughter

Not long after starting this work with older people I had a most difficult encounter. I was asked to see an 82 year-old woman, Mrs Hill, who had recovered from a stroke. She still managed to live alone in her home owing to regular visits by her two daughters who lived nearby. She was getting more and more angry with the daughters when they came to help and the situation was becoming intolerable for them all. Her elder daughter, a woman in her late forties, brought Mrs Hill who, a little unsteadily, walked with the daughter's assistance into my office. Mrs Hill was a large rotund woman, with many chins, and wisps of grey hair falling around her face. She wore a shapeless cotton dress. Her daughter explained her mother was very hard of hearing, so it would be better if she stayed with us. I agreed but started to feel uneasy. When they sat down Mrs Hill took out her false teeth and then her hearing aid, complaining that both were uncomfortable.

Whatever I said, however loud I shouted, Mrs Hill was unable to hear me. Sometimes she put her hearing aid back in her ear, but it made no difference. She could however understand what her daughter said. With the daughter as a kind of interpreter I asked her to tell me something about herself. She spoke about her husband who had died a few years previously. It was an unhappy marriage. He spent most of his spare time at the pub. She described preparing dinner and then waiting with the girls for her husband to come home to eat it. They waited with some dread because he could be unpleasant.

I shouted various questions. Each time she only seemed to hear when her daughter repeated what I'd said. Almost as an afterthought Mrs Hill mentioned that this was a second marriage. She had a previous marriage just before the outbreak of the Second World War. Her first husband had enlisted and disappeared during the war. She waited for him for three years. He was never found. At the top of my voice I shouted 'I think you feel you've spent most of your life waiting!' Mrs Hill looked blankly at me. I repeated myself trying more loudly, feeling desperate to make myself understood but to no avail. I asked her daughter to repeat this interpretation. Mrs Hill beamed a toothless grin and slapped her thigh with glee, saying to me: 'Now you're talking!'

Later, I added that I thought each time she waited for her daughters to visit she was reminded of the other times when she waited for her two husbands. She returned to talking of her regrets about the marriage to her second husband. She was particularly unhappy about the way he treated her daughters. It seemed he was cruel to them. At this point Mrs Hill's daughter became upset and angry, telling me she didn't want to talk about her father or think about him anymore. It was drawing near the end of the hour and I offered to see them again. Mrs Hill looked interested to come back, but I could see that her daughter did not agree. They did not return.

Fifteen months later I was told that Mrs Hill had suffered a second stroke, she could no longer speak or swallow food and she was to go into a nursing home. I was asked to see her daughters because the staff on the rehabilitation ward felt they were finding it 'difficult to stand back'. When I saw the daughters they complained bitterly that the doctor on the ward told them they were 'too tied to their mother and visited her too often'. They were very angry. I said that perhaps they also felt angry with me following my meeting with Mrs Hill the previous year. They agreed. The elder daughter said she and her mother were upset for some days after the meeting. She added that there was no point in getting upset, it was all in the past. The younger daughter then talked about her suspicions about the hospital. They had to make frequent visits to keep a check on what the staff were doing. They were unhappy because the staff 'threatened' that they would send Mrs Hill to a nursing home and hadn't told them. They emphasised that their mother had had a hard and unhappy life. I said I felt they were trying to make it up to her. They agreed and seemed to soften in their attitude, speaking more calmly and with some resignation about the likelihood of Mrs Hill going to a nursing home.

## Commentary

When Freud's patient Dora, who was 18, broke off treatment prematurely, Freud wrote that her father gave him assurances that she would return. Freud doubted this because he suspected that Dora's father was only interested in the therapy so long as Freud did what the father wanted, which Freud was not willing to do (Freud, 1905a). As with the young, therapy with older people is often dependent on the co-operation of relatives. Despite her hearing problems I felt I made a good contact with Mrs Hill. I think in my counter-transference I experienced something of how desperate she felt. She was delighted to be understood and eager to talk about her unhappiness. It was however an upsetting meeting. In the daughter's transference to me I became the cruel father inflicting pain on her and her mother. Ironically I was trying to show them that Mrs Hill's anger with her daughters when they visited, was the anger transferred onto the daughters about the two husbands who had kept her waiting. In other words, contrary to the daughter's objection that it was all in the past, because of Mrs Hill's transference onto her daughters when she felt abandoned by them, the past anger was being experienced in the present. The painfulness of this exploration with the daughters gave real hooks for a negative paternal transference to me.

I was also puzzled that no matter how hard I tried Mrs Hill could only hear her daughter. Even when it was clear Mrs Hill wished to return for more counselling and her daughter didn't, I felt I couldn't prise them apart. Later, the somewhat curious referral from the rehabilitation ward, that the daughters couldn't stand back, seems to reflect something of the same process: though they could no longer look after their mother they could not let her go to a nursing home.

I interpreted the daughters' opening remarks about their anger with the rehabilitation doctor to be an expression of their negative transference to me. This interpretation was confirmed when they were then able to express their anger with me. This is an example of a split transference, in which the client(s) in talking angrily about some outside person can be splitting off their anger in the transference about the therapist. The negative feelings need to be gathered into the transference onto the therapist in order for the ambivalent feelings to be worked through. It is of course tempting for the therapist to retain this split, not to have to face the client's anger and apparently be favoured as the good guy in contrast to the baddies elsewhere.

I think the daughters' anger with me, with the doctor, who was female and their suspicions of staff on the ward, were all expressing a negative transference of a father who was trying to prise them apart from their mother. (Different transferences can occur irrespective of the gender or age of the therapist.) It is likely that Mrs Hill's second husband, who seemed such a poor husband and father, did not help these girls separate from their mother, or her from them, instead he made them close allies against a common enemy, bound together by their anger at his abandonment. My successful interpretation to Mrs Hill threatened this alliance by making a link with her with which she was delighted, but which upset her daughter because at that moment I was coming between them like a father who has a special relationship with a mother. The daughters had separated from their mother and established families of their own. However, their mother's deteriorating physical condition and the increasing reality of her likely death, doubtless revived the daughters' infantile fears of maternal loss and abandonment. Reciprocally, for Mrs Hill the grief about her strokes, the regrets about her married life, the loss of her home and her encroaching death, led her to cling to her daughters as a life raft and to hear only her daughter's voice. When I could acknowledge the daughters' loving and reparative feelings, that they were trying to make up for their mother's unhappiness, it supported their adult concern for their mother and seemed to help them accept the plans for her future care.

## Summary

Brief interventions of a very few sessions, particularly in the context of older people suffering losses associated with physical illness and incapacity, can provide some understanding about the implications for the older person's internal and external worlds, and enable mourning about the consequences of the losses. It is especially important to register the shock which is often a powerful part of a bereavement reaction to illness and disability, doubtless connected with a bodily narcissism and a profound belief that the body will never falter or fail. Feelings of bereavement also include panic, denial, guilt and anger.

Including partners, other family members or carers in the therapy can be beneficial in supporting loving and caring relationships, but may prove difficult because of shared problems about grieving, and because of the older person's dependency on family members who can obstruct therapy. Nonetheless these interventions may provide an opportunity to gather in and ease negative feelings transferred onto the family or treatment team. Sometimes this means attending to a split transference in which the therapist may be favoured with benign feelings in contrast to others with whom there is much strife, or vice versa. Recognising infantile fears which are stirred by the incapacity or likely death of a parent may support family members and help them support their parents.

# 3
# LONGER INDIVIDUAL THERAPY

## Introduction

This chapter illustrates some key issues in ageing which emerged from a longer therapy with two clients. For Mrs Taylor there were particular difficulties about dependency when she suddenly became ill. For Mr Krol the awareness of ageing and the nearness of death brought an urgency to try to digest a terrible trauma which he had not been able to speak about before. The chapter concludes with some comments about therapy and sexual trauma suffered by older people.

These clients are presented in extended case studies, examples of which continue in the next three chapters. The value of lingering over the detail of the moment by moment, session by session contact is that it enables a study of the gradual unfolding of the transference and counter-transference relationship, and developments in the therapy. This form of study is like slowing down the speed of a film for a frame by frame view to better understand what is happening. It is similar to the detailed study of the interactions between client and therapist that is the usual procedure in psychodynamic supervision when a therapist brings accounts of particular sessions with a client for discussion with his or her supervisor.

## Dependency late in life

### Mrs Taylor – who collapsed into helplessness

This description of therapy with Mrs Taylor covers assessment meetings and 16 weekly sessions. The last two took place at her bedside in hospital, a fortnight before she died. It is an account of a woman who seemed, in remarkable ways, to have remained strong and fit until she entered her eighth decade and then suffered an abrupt decline. I have given excerpts from the sessions which show an awful dilemma: life had ceased to hold any purpose for this woman, she was impatient to die, but at the same time she feared dying.

## Infantilisation and fears of dependency

*At the beginning in the way the referral was accepted and then in the assessment meetings I was drawn into an infantilising attitude toward this older woman.*

Mrs Taylor was 80 years old. She was referred by a consultant physician from the general hospital who told me Mrs Taylor had recently been discharged from the acute ward where she had been admitted suffering from shingles, nausea and renal failure. There had been a fracas on the ward when her son had threatened the female consultant physician. Apparently he lived underneath his mother in a house which was divided into two flats. The consultant was worried about the relationship between mother and son. Mrs Taylor, who had been very active and out each day in the local shopping centre, was now 'hesitant and shaky'. She would certainly not be able to resume her active life. She was to return for an out-patient appointment when the consultant intended to refer her to me. I was informed of arrangements which could be made for her to have transport to bring her to my consulting room. I gave the consultant an appointment to pass on to Mrs Taylor when she saw her. The appointment was subsequently cancelled because Mrs Taylor was readmitted to hospital.

I did not hear about her again until five months later when Mrs Taylor's GP contacted my secretary and asked if she could be given another appointment. Mrs Taylor attended this appointment with her daughter-in-law. She came into my office shuffling in tiny steps, leaning heavily on her daughter-in-law's arm. It was a cold wintry day in late February and she was wearing a long grey overcoat with large buttons all the way down. She stood struggling to unbutton the coat and looked appealing for help to her daughter-in-law, who appeared exasperated and reluctantly assisted with the buttons. Mrs Taylor sat down breathless. She was a slight figure, with thinning grey hair curled at the ends. She had rather large spectacles, bright eyes and was neatly dressed in a skirt, blouse and a cardigan. Her daughter-in-law sat alongside her making a sharp contrast, a tall angular woman with reddish hair, who, in a business-like manner, introduced herself and asked me if she could speak with me alone. Mrs Taylor remained silent. When I asked her about my seeing her daughter-in-law, she answered in a tremulous voice that she had no objection. So I agreed, saying that I would also like to see Mrs Taylor on her own after I had spoken with her daughter-in-law.

Once on her own the daughter-in-law launched into a tirade of complaints about Mrs Taylor. She said there had been a great change since her mother-in-law's illness because she had become frightened and dependent, a burden on her and her husband, who was Mrs Taylor's only child. Their life was now terribly constricted since Mrs Taylor wouldn't let them go anywhere without her. Furthermore, she suspected her mother-in-law of malingering because she would tell them she couldn't do anything for herself but they could hear her moving around quite agilely upstairs. When they appeared she would be on her sofa saying she couldn't move. She said her mother-in-law had a different story for everybody. I found this an extremely difficult interview. It was hard to stop the flood of complaints. I felt overwhelmed with the daughter-in-law's rage, almost suffocated by her.

When I saw Mrs Taylor she said she didn't mind talking to me. She said she had suffered badly with shingles and showed me where the shingles had affected her around the neck. She was very upset about feeling so weak and helpless, but she couldn't see how I could help her poor physical condition. I agreed that there wasn't much I could do about her physical state, but said it could be helpful to understand more about her feelings and how they might contribute to her physical problems. She seemed interested. I asked her about her life. She said little about herself simply that she'd had a good childhood and a poor marriage, but she didn't want to talk about her marriage.

At the end of these interviews I felt perplexed and still affected by the daughter-in-law's suffocating rage. I said that before I could make any recommendation about what might help, I would like to meet Mrs Taylor's son.

A fortnight later Mrs Taylor's son and daughter-in-law came to see me. I felt some apprehension after what I had heard about his threatening behaviour to the consultant. He was a thickset, intense man, in a black suit and carried a black leather briefcase. But he was mild-mannered and eager to talk about the problems with his mother. He told me his father had died 26 years ago. He left home shortly after; though later he built a two-storey house for himself with one floor for his mother. He said until her illness his mother had been caring, independent and likeable. She had often done the shopping for them and other household chores like washing and gardening. Now she was very dependent, couldn't be left alone and claimed not to be able to do anything. She seemed to feel too frail to lift a spoon, whereas once she had been formidable. She had run a factory, could do any manual job in it and used to lift heavy equipment. Even up to her eighties she was extremely active and looked younger than her years. After two strokes, she had managed to make a full recovery and resume life to the full.

As they talked, I again found the atmosphere of rage and persecution intolerable. I struggled to think. Finally I said I thought that Mrs Taylor appeared to have been quite an exceptional woman who had defied ageing, but now age and illness had caught up with her and perhaps she and they were afraid of her dying. The effect of this interpretation was like suddenly releasing air from a balloon, the tension dissipated. I felt I could bear to be in the room again. They both visibly relaxed a little. The further effect of the interpretation was that they brought new and important material. Mrs Taylor's daughter-in-law told me her mother-in-law had a fiancé, Jack, who hung himself because he had TB. Mrs Taylor had found him. Jack had given her an engagement ring which she had never removed until this latest time she was in hospital.

At the conclusion of this interview I offered to see Mrs Taylor for once weekly individual therapy of 50-minute sessions, provided she agreed. I proposed meeting with her for the next three weeks until my Easter holiday and to hold a review after Easter to see if she wanted to continue. Her daughter-in-law said she was willing to bring her each week.

## Commentary

In offering the consultant an appointment to give to Mrs Taylor I was drawn into a somewhat infantilising attitude. Instead, I could have asked Mrs Taylor to contact me for an appointment if she wished to pursue therapy, which would also have given some indication of her motivation. I was guilty of perpetuating an infantilising attitude, by treating her like a young child who had to wait outside while I talked to her daughter-in-law. Though this separate interview was requested by the daughter-in-law, my acquiescence led to an enactment of the very problems she complained about, because we were both acting as if her mother-in-law was unable to take part in an adult conversation. Excluding Mrs Taylor from the subsequent meeting with her son and daughter-in-law continued this enactment. Looking back, I can see that another aspect of this infantilisation is an expression of rage against a mother who becomes like a dependent child and who can mother no longer. This rather exceptional woman had looked after her son and daughter-in-law like a live-in housekeeper. They were furious and disbelieving that she could not continue doing so. To exclude her from these meetings was to collude in an attack on her adult self by only seeing her as a dependent child, and avoided the pain of thinking about an adult woman who suffered the humiliation of being reduced to a childlike state.

Infantilisation of older people embarrassing to see in my own behaviour and all too common in my experience of care with older people, reflects a form of defensive splitting and projective identification. When these older clients are treated like children the staff split off their own dependency and project it into the older people. Faced with an older client who may stir fears of a parent dying, infantilisation enables staff to evacuate their own infantile terrors. An alternative and complementary split that also occurred was when the staff tended to see their clients as rather uniformly old. For example staff were often surprised when I asked *how* old the patients were. These splits keep staff and patient separate and remove the staff from worries arising from feeling more identified with the patients, especially fears that as they age, one day they too might suffer these debilitating illnesses and face their own death.

The angry suspicion of the son and daughter-in-law that Mrs Taylor was lying about her disability avoided acknowledging the frightening implications of her illness. I did not take up their anger with her. In retrospect I think it was well that I didn't because such an interpretation could have felt like a criticism and contributed to an avoidance of deeper worries. The interpretation I offered reached fears about Mrs Taylor dying, and implicitly the infantile terror of mother dying. The validity and important effects of this interpretation were shown in a visible reduction of tension, and that they were more able to be in touch with their adult concern and think about Mrs Taylor's feelings. More useful information emerged. Some light was shed on how Mrs Taylor's experience of a debilitating illness may have revived the tragic loss of her fiancé. I felt I had a basis on which to proceed. However, my interview with Mrs Taylor had not been too promising, so it felt better to make a tentative arrangement which would allow her, and me, to see if therapy could be helpful to her.

It was clear that Mrs Taylor needed something private for herself, but in retrospect it would have been useful to have considered whether her son and daughter-in-law could have met with another therapist, to work in parallel with and thereby support my therapy with Mrs Taylor. I could have questioned the arrangement for the daughter-in-law to bring Mrs Taylor and whether separate transport would have been possible in order to give Mrs Taylor more independence about attending the sessions. (For a discussion of the assessment process in therapy see Noonan, 1983, pp. 48–63).

## Settling in

*The early sessions include a procedure often used in therapy: a trial period to allow more time for an assessment of the client, and to explore the feasibility of offering longer work. This process enables client and therapist to make more informed decisions, but also needs monitoring for the feelings it may stir in the client.*

At the first session Mrs Taylor shuffled somewhat breathlessly into the room. I decided not to assist her and simply to wait. But as she struggled to undo the large buttons of her grey overcoat I felt impelled to help her with them and hang the coat for her. She thanked me for seeing her. I explained about meeting for the next three weeks and then reviewing the situation after Easter. I said the meetings were an opportunity to talk about whatever she wished and that it could be helpful to bring any dreams if she remembered them. She then told me she had been incontinent, that she had no strength and couldn't get a grip on things. She became upset as she told me about how lonely and inactive she felt, spending much of the time on her own except for going three days each week to a day centre for the elderly.

Mrs Taylor said she felt hurt because her son was not affectionate to her. She would have liked him to kiss her and hold her hand. Then she talked of Jack whom she knew in her early twenties and to whom she had felt very close, but he died from TB. Later, when she was 29 she married her husband, Bill. He died when she was in her fifties. I saw a flash of her wit as, with a twinkle in her eye, referring to her marriage she quipped 'a late start and an early finish'. Bill was a heavy drinker, and, to her shame, he was frequently 'incontinent', wetting their bed. She felt angry and hurt. I wondered to myself whether her husband felt she loved only Jack.

In the second session Mrs Taylor told me of another man, Tom, who had been her fiancé. He became depressed because he lost his job. He had taken poison and then cut his throat. He was found dead on a path which was their favourite walk. Her hands shook as she spoke of this tragedy. I felt somewhat confused because of the slightly different account her daughter-in-law had given me in which Jack and Tom were fused together. When I asked about Jack, Mrs Taylor said she had known him before Tom, but because of his illness they could only be friends. After he knew he was dying from TB he gave her some money to buy a piece of jewellery to remember him. She bought a diamond ring which she wore on her little finger.

In the third session Mrs Taylor went over some of this history again. I ventured an interpretation that she felt guilty and responsible for the deaths of the three men who had been close to her. She looked rather quizzically at me, and said no, she didn't think she felt like that.

## Commentary

I can see from the start I felt in a dilemma of how much to help Mrs Taylor as she entered the room. Whilst I didn't feel I needed to assist her walking, I couldn't stand by and not help her as she struggled to unbutton her coat. There remained doubts in my mind whether these were genuine difficulties or attempts to manipulate me. I was afraid of escalating demands from this apparently helpless old woman. I felt by not helping her I might be suspicious and punitive like her son and daughter-in-law, or manipulated and foolish if I did. What was most frightening to Mrs Taylor, her family and me was her increasing sense of helplessness and dependency. The suspicions of malingering or manipulation, which may have been provoked by Mrs Taylor, offered a way of denying her frailty and implied that she was not helpless but still in control. However, when Mrs Taylor spoke of her incontinence and that she couldn't get a grip on things, I think she vividly conveyed her worries about no longer being able to hold herself together.

My experience of work with older people has confirmed a pattern in which people like Mrs Taylor who have often led exceptional lives, in old age can suddenly become psychologically debilitated by the onset of a physical illness or other intimations of dependency. The psychoanalyst Brian Martindale (1989a) has shed light on the underlying process. He describes the experience of becoming 'dependent again' in old age as presenting particular problems when there have been failures in the dependency relationship early in life. The approach of dependency heralded by the decline in physical and mental capacities brings a revival of fears that once again dependent needs will not be met. Discoveries in psychoanalytic infant observation help us understand more about the catastrophic anxieties associated with fears of dependency. Bick (1968) showed how important it is that the infant be sufficiently held by mother or primary caretaker, meaning physically as well as mentally held in mind. If there are prolonged experiences of being unheld then the infant will experience *unintegration*, which Bick and others have articulated as a terror of 'falling to pieces' or 'dissolving into space'. Thus in its earliest resonances a fear of dependency can reflect a dread of unintegration. Bick understood that when there has been insufficient holding the infant and then the child may develop ways of holding him- or herself together in premature ways like using its own body or mind in the absence of an internal sense of containment. I think these previously remarkable older people like Mrs Taylor who collapse into helplessness probably held themselves together and avoided depending on others until these defences were punctured by painful reminders of vulnerability and dependency which triggered terrors about falling to pieces.

The early sessions were time for Mrs Taylor to settle in, though it was difficult starting with just three weeks before a holiday. I was impressed that she was soon able to tell me about her husband in spite of her shame, but I think I became rather incontinent in an ill-timed interpretation about her guilt. It would have been better to have offered some understanding of her fear that she was falling apart, and of her loneliness that there was no one else she could talk to about her unhappiness. It could have been helpful too to acknowledge that she was probably wary of starting to depend on me because I was soon to abandon her during my holiday, reminiscent of how she had been let down by other men. The arrangement to have a review after the Easter holiday gave her the choice of whether to continue therapy with me or not, but she could have felt it was an opportunity for me give up on her.

### Anger and sorrow

*As the work progressed Mrs Taylor was able to express more of her anger. However, I had difficulty in taking up her angry feelings in relation to myself in the transference.*

Following the Easter break Mrs Taylor came back saying she had nothing to talk about, she'd told me everything. Then, in exasperation she held up her hands, saying they shouldn't be soft and clean like that. She used to do all the gardening, washing and ironing. Now she was frightened to be left alone at night. She was a burden on her son and daughter-in-law. She lay on her sofa every day, exhausted and breathless, unable to do anything. She had no energy and felt tense all the time, not knowing what she was tense about.

I asked about her parents and her family life. She brightened up a bit as she talked about her mother who was generous and kind, and whom she cared for when she was dying. Her mother lost her memory, could not walk and was incontinent. Mrs Taylor brought her mother home and slept on a day bed in the same room with her. It meant her son, who was 15 at the time, no longer had a room of his own but had to share with his father. She felt she neglected her son and he resented it. Her father had died some years before. She was very attached to him. Towards the end of the session I raised the question of how she felt about continuing therapy. She said she felt I was the only one she could speak to about these matters and she wanted to continue. I agreed that we could meet for as long as seemed useful. I said she or I could raise the question of finishing for us to discuss and hopefully agree about, but whenever we decided to finish it would need some time, at least a month's notice, to work on together. (It is now somewhat unusual to be able to offer open-ended therapy in the National Health Service, but early in my work with older people, my clinical psychology manager had agreed I could take on a few clients for open-ended work as a way of researching and deepening my understanding of older people.)

At the following fifth session, Mrs Taylor complained of finding it harder to walk. She brought a dream in which her mother and father were quarrelling because they had no money. She offered to give them some of her money but she found she had none. When she went upstairs to see if she could find any she saw her old friend Mabel ill in bed being looked after by another friend Dorothy. When I asked Mrs Taylor what the dream reminded her of, she talked about times when she had no money. She didn't borrow any because it wasn't done then, not like now when people have it so easy. Her friends Mabel and Dorothy used to work together in a factory with her. In an interpretation about the dream I picked up the anger in the quarrel by talking about her anger about feeling so depleted. She then spoke of the problems with her heart and kidneys. She was too old for dialysis because it needs to be given to the youngsters. Rather sorrowfully, she said nothing could be done about her heart.

Mrs Taylor then recalled my talking of her resentful feelings about not being able to do anything. Looking distressed, she said a few days ago she was nasty to her brother and sister when they came to visit her. They had been away at a seaside town where she used to go with them when she had been well. She'd scolded them saying 'You've been gadding about, not bothering about me!' She said she felt so resentful about so many things, repeatedly asking herself 'Why has this happened to me?' I said I felt she was waiting to die, to which she quickly replied 'God will take me when He's ready'. I thought she felt God was punishing her by keeping her waiting and she was tormented with questions about why He did so. Mrs Taylor said she did not fear death but more the way she might die. She worried that she would become more physically disabled and suffer a slow death.

In the sixth and seventh sessions Mrs Taylor continued to express an intense anger about what had happened to her. Her breathing difficulties also increased and sometimes appeared in the sessions when she would have to stop talking. She then seemed to be gasping for breath, though she soon recovered. Much of her anger was directed against her son and daughter-in-law because they kept insisting that she should be more independent. But her understanding from the doctor was that she wouldn't get any better. She was regretful about being a burden on her son and daughter-in-law and began to see that her resentment made them resentful. I said that her fears about being left alone prevented her son and daughter-in-law from going out on their own and kept them in the house just as she was confined in it. She replied she didn't mean to put a 'stopper' on their lives, it wasn't deliberate. They spent less and less time with her. She was furious because she felt they kept fobbing her off with stories about how busy they were in order to avoid being with her. There were plans for them to take her away for a weekend with an old friend of hers whom she had not seen for a very long time. At the last minute the son cancelled the plans because of work. She was terribly hurt. I felt angry and sorry too.

## Commentary

The Easter holiday break catalysed feelings about loss and abandonment and brought a strong negative transference into the therapy relationship, which enabled Mrs Taylor to express some of her rage and frustration. For a while my difficulty was in gathering up these angry feelings in relation to myself in the transference. For example unconsciously she felt I had been gadding about during the holiday, like her brother and sister, with no interest in her and, like her son and daughter-in-law, I did not want to spend time with her. Mrs Taylor's envy of me was appropriate because, unlike her, I could come and go. Ruth Porter, who has written of individual psychoanalytic psychotherapy with older patients, points out the need to recognise 'envy that is appropriate to the therapist' (1991, p. 485) because the therapist is mobile and independent. Angry or envious feelings are not easily expressed by someone who is weak and dependent, nor are such feelings welcome in most professional care settings or amongst families. It is important for elderly clients to be able to express anger because, as Porter has pointed out, unexpressed anger can have damaging effects on the internal world and can inhibit mourning and forgiveness. Whereas when anger is expressed it can often bring about constructive results, especially if there are justified complaints, thus 'reinforcing hope and counteracting helplessness' (p. 477).

Anger is difficult and frightening for therapists too. Faced with Mrs Taylor's anger and envy, it was tempting to perpetuate a split transference by not drawing the anger onto myself and then I could remain a nice therapist, in contrast to the others whom she riled against. When I took up some of her anger in the dream in relation to others, she was able to be in touch with some sorrowful feelings connected with her heart which nothing could be done about – perhaps a reference to her loving feelings which may have felt so injurious to the men in her life. However, by not linking her angry feelings with myself in the transference, I failed to take up her worries in the here-and-now of our relationship about the damaging effects of her destructive feelings on me. Nor at the time did I appreciate that her anger was also very likely a way of trying to survive, a way of trying again to hold herself together when her infantile self felt so frightened of falling to pieces or spilling out like her incontinence (Symington, 1985).

I took some of the sessions to supervision. My supervisor thought Mrs Taylor felt like a helpless little child who feared nobody loved or wanted her, and her adult self was in a rage about being reduced back to a childlike condition. She described Mrs Taylor's infantile fears in the dream, that she was trying to put it right for mummy and daddy but felt she couldn't; and that she felt like a child asking where do the good things come from, a child who was asking for more because she was so frightened she would not get enough, manifest in her gasping for breath. Martindale (2007) sees that underlying fears of dying are early experiences of failed dependency and fears that once again dependency needs will not be met. Mrs Taylor was clear that she was not afraid of death, but was fearful of dying in a slow and painful way, as though she did not expect to get the care she needed. These fears were confirmed when her son and daughter-in-law were rejecting and disappointing her. It is possible that Mrs Taylor unconsciously evoked such rejection in a projective process in which an internal abandoning figure is externalised in a transference relationship with others – or what Freud (1914) described as repeating rather than remembering.

My supervisor drew my attention to Mabel and Dorothy in the dream, signalling Mrs Taylor's longing for some contemporaries, most of whom were probably dead; and that Mrs Taylor could feel that when I saw her, unlike a friend, it was because it was my job. Supervision helped me to think about the negative transference expressed in the rage about her son and daughter-in-law and supported me in gathering these feelings into the therapeutic relationship. The importance of working with these negative feelings in the transference was to relieve Mrs Taylor's external relationships from such feelings.

## Closeness and loss

*The final period of the therapy which includes a summer holiday and a change of session time, illustrates how feelings about separation and loss are galvanised by breaks or changes in arrangements. The last sessions at the hospital bedside bring death to the fore and reveal the importance of talking boldly about death.*

Over the next few weeks a pattern emerged in the sessions. Mrs Taylor would arrive walking with great difficulty and looking more and more drawn and dishevelled. Sometimes her hair was obviously uncombed. On one occasion, unusually, there was a stain of food on her blouse. She would sit down gasping for breath, but after a few minutes she would recover and clearly be pleased to be with me. I vividly recall her describing a lunch at the day centre where they had served up a vegetable pie and included the same vegetables in the pie as side vegetables. I could see she felt anything could be served up to the old folks who wouldn't know the difference. I interpreted negative feelings more consistently in the transference. She was usually reluctant to think that she had any negative feelings towards me, needing to keep some splitting and see me as a somewhat idealised figure.

By now it was early summer. There were some lovely moments of contact between us when she would pause as afternoon sunlight entered the room, listening to a bird that sang on a rooftop nearby. She recognised it as a blackbird, a bird she was particularly fond of. I was pleased to learn about the blackbird and enjoyed the birdsong with her. However, I was troubled by Mrs Taylor's worsening physical condition. Though she had been seen by her GP, little seemed to have been done for her. I spoke with the consultant physician again to gain some more clarification of Mrs Taylor's state of health. The consultant confirmed that Mrs Taylor was in a genuinely poor physical state but she was still puzzled why Mrs Taylor was quite so weak.

At the end of June, in the twelfth session, Mrs Taylor told me her son and daughter-in-law had arranged a two-week summer holiday during which she was to go into a local nursing home, in the last week of July and the first week of August. I told her I would be away for the month of August. A week later I had to rearrange the day of the session a fortnight ahead. In the rest of the session she was very angry, describing herself as 'an old rag' and an imbecile because of the way her son and daughter-in-law kept things from her. I took up her rage with myself who didn't tell her why there had to be a change of day for the session time, or about my holiday. I said that she suspected I wanted to get away from an old rag. She replied with a sparkle in her eye and a smile 'Whether you like it or not, I'm coming!'

Mrs Taylor's anger increased. In the thirteenth session she said she'd had a row with her son. In the fourteenth session she came in a fragile state, so much so that, unusually, her daughter-in-law stayed in the waiting area while her mother-in-law was with me. The next session was the one I had rescheduled for a different day. Mrs Taylor did not turn up. I had a message that she had been admitted to the general hospital. I learned that she was admitted because she was in a weak state. The following week I sent a message that I would visit her at the usual time and day of her session.

On my way to see her I spoke to the nursing staff. They seemed surprised that Mrs Taylor was still alive, but they couldn't understand why she had come back into hospital because she looked no worse than before. Mrs Taylor had a single room. When I entered she was sitting up in bed, supported by several pillows. There was an oxygen cylinder and mask alongside her. I sat in a chair beside her bed. She closed her eyes, remained silent and seemed to be trying to fall asleep. I felt I was being given the cold shoulder, but I wondered too if my presence meant she felt more comfortable and then could allow herself to sleep. Then I became preoccupied with watching her breathing, fearing she might die at any moment. I talked to her about her anger with me for changing the session time and for leaving her during my holiday. I said that getting herself admitted to hospital ensured she would be looked after 24 hours a day in contrast to my inadequate care. She looked interested in the interpretation, but then closed her eyes. I started worrying about her breathing, again fearful she might die. I also had a fantasy that she was deliberately holding her breath. I talked about her fear that she might die, and linked it with her feeling that I dropped her when I left her. She again told me God would take her when He was ready. But this time she added that nobody had come back from the grave to say what it was like. During the silences which followed I was uncomfortable to find myself thinking about what I would do with her session time if she died. So I said that she might feel I was waiting for her to die so I could get on with something else. She said she was waiting and wondering, but she did not say more about what she meant.

The next week was the final week before my holiday. Mrs Taylor was still in hospital and I went to see her at the usual time. Apparently there had been no change in her condition. When I arrived she was sitting up in bed watching television. Almost reluctantly she turned the television off and looked at me. For some time she said nothing. I noticed she was breathing in very short breaths in a panicky way. I talked to her about her panic that she would die. She tended to lapse into silence still breathing in short breaths. Only towards the end of the session did she give some acknowledgment of the interpretations, with some humour agreeing she had moaned at me about my holiday. She also commented on the way the furniture had been placed in the room, a wardrobe that hadn't been centred properly and floor tiles which had been inexpertly laid. With some pride she told me she wouldn't have done it like that.

She had a plate of sandwiches in front of her and explained that she hadn't eaten them because her son was bringing some special food which her daughter-in-law had prepared for her. Just as we were near the end of the session she looked at me rather mischievously and took a bite from one of the sandwiches. I said I felt she didn't think much of what I'd offered her, the sandwich was a better bet. Her eyes lit up, she smiled and said 'Well, there's the door!' It was nearly time to finish, I reminded her when I would resume after the holiday and bade her farewell. When I returned from holiday I learned that Mrs Taylor died in hospital, a fortnight after I last saw her. I was shocked and very sad. I wrote to her son and daughter-in-law to express my sorrow, offering to see them if they wished. They did not reply. I missed seeing Mrs Taylor for a long while after.

## Commentary

It seemed to me Mrs Taylor got into an increasing panic about dying. As indicated earlier these fears of dying reflect an unconscious terror of failed dependency and being dropped, and they were very likely intensified by the anticipation of her son's holiday which overlapped with mine. The change of session time was disturbing and another disruption to the holding provided by the continuity and regularity of therapeutic arrangements. Again her anger may have been a way of holding herself together. However, when Mrs Taylor felt I understood some of her fears she felt held in my mind, her panic temporarily subsided, she was able to breathe normally and enjoy the blackbird's song. Listening to the song may also have found unconscious echoes in feeling held while listening as an infant to mother's voice.

The reason for not disclosing information about the change of session time or about my holiday was to keep some space in which to think about the conscious and especially the unconscious phantasies that were stirred by these events. There is no golden rule about whether to offer explanations or not, except keeping the interests of the client in mind. It is important to be aware of wanting to avoid a client's wrath by offering a good excuse. Even if an explanation is given, there may still be lingering feelings and phantasies, but giving a reason may make it more difficult to gain access to the feelings and phantasies. Sensitivity to feelings stirred by holidays or changes in arrangements is important for carers, as well as therapists, as they come and go in the lives of their older clients.

During the last two sessions in hospital, which were the final weeks of Mrs Taylor's life, her remoteness from me may have been a form of 'anticipatory mourning' as she prepared to die. Dorothy Judd describes anticipatory mourning, (citing work by Eissler), as a process in which someone who is dying 'gradually detaches from his loved ones as a way of easing separation before death' (1989, p. 147). Judd points out that because family and relatives have a strong wish for the patient to survive, a therapist may be in a better position to allow this process of anticipatory mourning to happen. The transference relationship can thus be 'a substitute arena for the relinquished ties' (p. 147). Another aspect of my fears about Mrs Taylor which Judd's work illuminates is her understanding that for those involved with the dying, alongside conscious feelings of guilt and failure, there are also 'primitive phantasies' of unconscious impulses of hatred towards loved ones from early life, which can lead to feelings of being responsible for the death. From this point of view my panic at Mrs Taylor's bedside probably reflected underlying phantasies in which I felt it would be my fault if she died.

Mrs Taylor was tormented by loneliness. Following some moments of closeness she shared with me, I felt she was then able to experience her loneliness in a less persecuted and more sad and resigned way. Gabriele Pasquali (1993) describes a loneliness that follows the experience of real intimacy as 'a loneliness felt to be without remedy'. As her physical frailty worsened there was an intensification of her fears that she had no internal resources and there would be no one to care for her. She experienced such fears concretely as not having enough breath, the breath of life. When I could take up her angry feelings in the transference, even though she could not consciously accept the interpretations, she was in touch again with robust external and internal figures, and felt held. She came to life in unexpected ways, showing humour and vitality, because at those moments I was able to think about and withstand her anger and wit.

## Long term effects of severe trauma

### Mr Krol – a survivor of a concentration camp

Mr Krol, a 72 year-old Polish man, was referred to me by his GP. The GP wrote that Mr Krol had a long history of anxiety and panic attacks, connected with wartime experiences in a concentration camp. Recently he had become embroiled in conflict where he lived which had made him extremely fearful. It was with some trepidation that I invited Mr Krol for an initial assessment with a view to therapy because I had not anticipated I would be called upon to work with survivors of the concentration camps. In my naiveté, a defensive innocence, I had assumed that the survivors would be too old or already dead.

## Difficulties in beginning to talk about trauma

*The early sessions with Mr Krol helped him overcome his profound difficulties in talking about his experiences in the concentration camp. This therapy is a reminder of the trauma many older people suffer through war experiences and provides some insight into how trauma of whatever kind, has lasting effects into old age.*

Mr Krol arrived punctually, a debonair man, with a ready smile and a distinctive continental charm. He spoke with a slight accent, but was fluent and rarely hesitated for the word he wanted. I particularly noticed his clothes because he was carefully dressed in rather lively colours, wearing a smart checked shirt with a well-matched tie. He talked at length about problems with a new flat he had recently moved to. He was very unhappy there. Much of his distress was focussed on the residents' car park which was alongside his flat. The car park was near a shopping centre and was being used by non-residents, especially young people, who disturbed him during the night as they arrived or departed. He had gone out to remonstrate with a group who then verbally abused and threatened him. He was shaken up by it. Although he was making representation to the authorities about protecting the car park, he felt pessimistic that anything would be done. He regretted having moved to the flat. He felt more and more tormented by living there. He had decided to try to move again which filled him with apprehension.

Somewhat reluctantly he mentioned a bit about the rest of his life. He described a lonely, unhappy life. He had never spoken to anyone about the concentration camp. He doubted that he would be able to do so now. Nonetheless I felt he could see a connection between the torment he suffered in his new flat and the persecution in the camp. I thought he now desperately needed to talk about the concentration camp before he died. I felt this could be long and difficult work, so I was glad to be able to offer him open-ended therapy. I sensed his readiness to begin and felt no need to build in a review after a few sessions. He accepted my offer of once weekly therapy. I think he felt relieved but also frightened, and so did I.

During the following three weeks Mr Krol talked about his life before and after the war, but said little about the concentration camp.

I learned he was born into a poor family, with an older sister who was his sole surviving relative and two brothers who were dead. When he was just five years old, his father, who worked in a foundry facing a hot furnace with his back exposed to the cold, died of pneumonia. He had no memories of his father, except when father was ill he'd been told that when father recovered he was in for a good hiding. He described his mother as cold and strict. He recalled her wanting him to sit on her lap and him running away afraid of her. Late in her life his mother told him that when she was in her teens she was raped. His few happy memories seemed to be of school, though he also said he played truant a great deal. He had started an apprenticeship just before the outbreak of war. Then he was incarcerated in Auschwitz because he had refused to join the German army. After two and a half years he was released.

He eventually made his way to England where he lived ever since. He had had no stable relationships. He had fathered a son by a woman who married another man and took the boy to live abroad. He never saw his son again. From another brief relationship he had a daughter. She was then raised by her mother and a step-father. In later years, when his daughter contacted him he discovered she had suffered abuse by the step-father. She lived as a single parent with a son of her own. She was interested to establish a relationship with Mr Krol. He could hardly bring himself to see her. In his forties he had a break-down and slashed his wrists. When his wrists were being stitched the doctor told him it would hurt, he replied that he couldn't be hurt anymore. Recently Mr Krol had become involved with a widow 11 years younger. They met in a therapy group. He subsequently left the group because he couldn't talk about his experiences. He spent a lot of time with this woman, and helped her decorate her maisonette. Later, when her daughter moved out, he sometimes used to stay with her.

He described just one experience in the concentration camp. He said he had felt determined to survive. He focussed all his effort on acquiring food because he knew that he would perish on the rations that were provided. He recalled running to a van which was delivering some hot food. He grabbed a bundle of potatoes and hid them under his shirt. He did not notice they were hot, or realise until afterwards that they burnt his flesh.

Mr Krol remained reluctant to say more about the concentration camp. He preferred talking about his childhood and thinking about how his later difficulties might be connected with his early life. Throughout these first sessions there was a recurring theme which suggested he feared he or I would not be able to bear being exposed to his memories of the camp. For example in the third session he spoke of feeling sorely let down after the war. He had held onto the hope in the camp of one day being free and able to return to Poland, but it was taken over by communism. Whilst acknowledging his bitterness and sadness that he had not been able to return to his country, I also talked to him about his hope for the therapy, that it would provide an opportunity to talk and his fear that I would let him down and not be able to bear the pain of his experiences. (There were of course grounds for his fears because already the brief glimpse he had given me of the camp had been distressing for both of us.) After this interpretation he recalled another occasion in the camp when he had tried to pick up a baked potato which had fallen on the ground. Three times he tried to get the potato and each time he was caught and beaten. Finally the guard crushed the potato underfoot. Mr Krol said he learned not to yell when he was beaten because those who yelled were beaten all the more.

Four weeks later Mr Krol began telling me more about his experiences in the camp. He was just 20 when the province in which he lived was annexed by the Germans and the young men were expected to join the German army. He refused to enlist. His mother was against him joining the Germans to fight their war. The Gestapo came for him at 4.00am. He remembered his mother crying and pleading with them to take her instead. After two days in a police station he was taken to Auschwitz to make an example of him for failing to join the army. Conditions there were primitive, a pump in the open for washing in summer and winter. He had to push wheelbarrows along planks and recalled having to run when the wheelbarrows were empty. They were squeezed into barracks with a German prisoner in charge. On arrival they were routinely beaten. He did not utter a sound, and because of this he thought they beat him less. When he stole food, though they beat him, he wasn't reported. He told me again how he dashed to the containers of steaming potatoes and hid some under his shirt, oblivious to the burning heat, determined only to survive.

After 16 months he was 'lucky' and got a job under shelter in a garage, spraying cars. It was an opportunity to escape but he didn't because he knew that if he did then 25 fellow prisoners would be taken as 'hostages' and killed. He also feared the consequences for his family. But, he asked, where would he have hidden anyway? When others escaped he used to stand stiffly to attention, looking the Germans straight in the eye, because he thought that perhaps in this way they would think he was strong, a good worker and would not take him as a hostage. During escapes they were kept standing all night. The bodies of those whose attempts to escape were unsuccessful, were put on display. He and others had to march past and look at them. They marched to music played by bands of inmates. Later, the camp looked like a sanatorium with decent buildings and avenues of trees. He saw the Jews arriving, mothers and children, told they were to take showers. The crematorium could not cope with the bodies. They were buried in mass graves.

I had to cancel the next week's session because I was ill. I felt I had 'flu. My overriding concern was about Mr Krol because he had just started talking about the camp. I felt my absence would fulfil his worst fears. It was unusual for me to be unwell. This was the first time since starting at the hospital nine months earlier, I had had to cancel appointments because of illness. I phoned Mr Krol to tell him I was unwell but hoped to see him for his next appointment. I recovered and was able to see him the following week. I had been deeply shocked and upset when he started to tell me more about the camp, but it was only later that I realised the connection between my illness and my feelings about hearing about the camp.

When we met the next week he resumed his account where he had left off. Later, he admitted he felt he was not able to convey to me what it was like in the camp. He feared I would think he was making it all up, or I would look upon what happened to him like the books or films that have been produced about the camps. It was an important moment when he realised that for much of the time in the camp he felt detached and looked on as though it wasn't real and he wasn't there. The reality of these experiences, the fear that he or I would break down because of the pain or be unaffected, remained issues we had to work through again and again.

## Commentary

I have included some of my work with Mr Krol to illustrate how trauma may finally need to be brought to therapy because of the fear of dying with the trauma undigested and still tormenting. The therapy illustrates some of the problems of trying to digest what may ulti- mately be indigestible. Especially in this early therapy with Mr Krol, I drew heavily on supervision and my own personal analysis, because I found the work so distressing. On first hearing of Mr Krol my super- visor spoke of the need to record his story. She didn't mean literally audio record it, but rather a sense she picked up that it needed to be made real, that he needed to tell his story. As she and I pieced his story together we could see how her reaction spoke too of the importance of his story being listened to and thought about. During the first eight weeks, when Mr Krol was unable to say much about the camp, I think what finally helped him to begin his story was that I was prepared to simply wait and think about his worries about talking of the camp. In this way I began to understand his worries through my counter-transference feelings of panic and dread.

My sudden illness and cancelled session after he started talking about the concentration camp reflected my difficulty in hearing about the trauma and processing it in my mind. Because of the suddenness of my absence I explained the reason to him, unlike the planned change to the arrangements with Mrs Taylor. The week's absence didn't seem to impede the subsequent work with him. However, I had to look out for and articulate his phantasy that he had damaged me and would do so again, especially as we approached holidays when he seemed to feel he had worn me out. My absence may have provided some reassurance that I could allow his trauma to have an impact on me; and even if it meant a temporary breakdown in containment, I could recover and return. Many months later, after a Christmas holiday, he said to me, with great feeling, referring to his reactions to the break, 'after all this, you *still* want to see me'. Throughout the work I worried about being overwhelmed with distress, or detaching myself and withdrawing from the pain.

Another aspect of Mr Krol's difficulties in talking about the camp was conveyed when he told me several times how he did not yell when the guards beat him because they would only beat him more if he did. I can now see that he was telling me about a negative transference, in which he feared if he gave expression to his hurt and pain then I would be cruel like the guards. Mr Krol was the last patient I saw in the evenings. On one occasion when I was the last to leave and responsible for locking the building, driving away in a hurry I became afraid I had locked Mr Krol in. I hadn't, but this experience brought home to me the power of the transference and counter-transference connected with a cruel incarceration.

The effects of war trauma are now classified as post-traumatic stress disorders. There is a considerable body of research which attests to the long term effects of post-traumatic stress disorders associated with war trauma, often exacerbated by ageing (for example Robbins, 1994). A study of former World War Two prisoners of war, found that 40 years later nearly a third suffered PTSD symptoms (Speed et al, 1989, quoted by Robbins). Caroline Garland has written about psycho-analytic work with patients suffering PTSD from various external dis-asters. Garland found that the long-term effects of trauma differ for each survivor because the trauma links up 'with whatever is damaged or flawed from the survivor's past' (Garland, 1991, p. 508). In particular, because the trauma is a catastrophic assault on life and on anyone's capacity to manage anxiety, it tends to reactivate earlier problems in the containing maternal relationship, including the more ordinary and inevitable flaws in such relationships. Hence trauma can damage an individual's subsequent capacity to manage anxiety, including the capacity to think symbolically and distinguish fantasy from reality. Consequently the trauma can be felt concretely to be the same as the original difficulties in containment. I think Mr Krol's account of the potatoes which burned his skin, may illustrate this concrete thinking: this memory conveys an internal state where something nourishing has become identified with something life-threatening. In other words the trauma of the concentration camp revived and became identified with, the early, probably ordinary lapses in maternal care. Despite Mr Krol's account of his mother's own trauma of being raped and that she was cold to him, it is not clear that there were exceptional difficulties in his early relationship with her. She did survive the rape just as he managed to survive the concentration camp.

In therapy with Mr Krol I aimed to enable him to tell the story about the concentration camp and to have a go at helping him manage trauma that was unthinkable and unbearable. The work involved was similar to the psychoanalytic psychotherapy with PTSD outlined by Garland (1991). It meant allowing him to tell his story again and again; helping him to distinguish the reality of the evil he had endured from the internal phantasies of cruelty and destructiveness it stirred in him, to which I was alerted through the counter-transference; and working with his guilt about having survived when so many perished, and his justified rage about what had happened to him. It also meant addressing earlier problems which were reactivated by the trauma of the concentration camp and repeatedly acknowledging his feeling that he would never get over what had happened to him. My hope was that the therapy would help him to feel free of some of the torment which contaminated his life, to feel less aggrieved and instead be able to feel sad about the irretrievable damage that had been done to his life. I hoped too he might be able to enjoy what was possible in the time that was left, even though what we might accomplish would fall short of what he and I wanted for him.

The therapy with Mr Krol reached a conclusion four years later. Near the end, as much to my surprise and delight as his own, he told me he was having the 'best time' of his life.

# Some comments about therapy and the trauma of sexual abuse

Just as reports of sexual abuse have become more prevalent amongst younger people, more older people now bring early experiences of sexual abuse to therapy. I have had contrasting experiences of working with sexual abuse suffered by older people. On the one hand the work was similar in many respects to the model of psychoanalytic psychotherapy for the aftermath of trauma described by Caroline Garland which I found useful in my work with Mr Krol. For example there was a need for longer term work, sometimes extending over a year or more, to go over the details of the abuse and the very painful feelings and conflicts about it, to unravel various aspects of the resulting trauma which had become entwined with other early or later problems, and to mourn the damaging effects of the trauma on the client's life.

On the other hand some therapeutic work with the trauma of sexual abuse may need to be brief, because longer therapy may reinforce persecuting ruminations and grievances. For example an older woman became preoccupied late in life with abuse she suffered as a young girl. The perpetrator of the abuse had died. She remained consumed with tormenting feelings of grievance, guilt and anger. The therapy was concluded after just four sessions at fortnightly intervals. What seemed important in this work was helping this woman see how these ruminations perpetuated an internal abuse. In other words she had internalised an abusive figure in her mind who kept blaming her, nurtured grievances and demanded retribution. She soon came to feel relieved of some of the burden of guilt and was less tormented. In the fourth session she said 'what a tangled web we weave'. I thought when she was able to see the web of grievances and accusations, and was thus less dominated by a spidery abusive figure, she was able to feel freer and have some hope about the rest of her life. Although I had offered further meetings, before the fifth meeting she contacted me to say she did not want to meet again or to continue to talk about the abuse. I thought this was an appropriate conclusion to the therapy.

## Summary

The case studies of longer therapeutic work illustrate problems of struggling with dependency in old age, and the need to finally speak about trauma before one dies. Mrs Taylor, a previously formidable woman, late in life collapsed into a helpless and dependent state. Early in the contact with Mrs Taylor fears of dependency can be seen communicated in the counter-transference, when there was an inclination to infantilise and project dependency into her or to feel worried about being controlled and manipulated by her as she struggled with helplessness. For a while it was difficult too to take up her anger in the transference, or to see that her anger was probably a way of her still trying to hold herself together, when faced with fears of being unheld and falling to pieces. Working with feelings stirred by breaks and holidays during the therapy were particularly valuable because they galvanise feelings about loss and abandonment, and fears of dying which are more troubling when there is a dread of dependency. When Mrs Taylor's feelings could be put into words, especially her fears and anger, then she felt held and in contact with strong internal and external figures. Being at her bedside not long before she died, gave me an opportunity to continue to help her face her fears; but also meant I needed to manage feelings of panic and guilt in myself.

Old age can bring an urgency to tell the untold story of a trauma that had been suffered earlier in life. Mr Krol suffered as a prisoner in a concentration camp but had not previously been able to talk about it. Central to his worries were that his traumatic experiences would be treated with disbelief and could not be borne or made more bearable for him. The need in this work is to recognise one's vulnerability, to have a go at bearing what may be unbearable, and hold the tension between being affected, perhaps losing one's therapeutic composure, but being able to recover and return to the work. The essence of the work means allowing the story to be told, and retold, at its own pace, remaining alert to what suffering and adversity in the external world can stir internally, particularly through careful monitoring of counter-transference feelings that may be hard to admit or accept. It is important too to understand how difficulties earlier in life may have linked up with trauma. Trying to manage trauma calls upon inner resources for containment of feelings which are established early in life, particularly in the mother-infant relationship. Excessive trauma is usually too much for any internal containment, and difficulties in assimilating the trauma may wrap around earlier problems in the maternal containing relationship, and even quite ordinary lapses in maternal care.

Often long-term therapeutic work is necessary to unravel the damage wrought by trauma. However, sometimes, especially in the context of early sexual abuse brought by older people, brief interventions may be appropriate in order to support the curtailment of an internal tormenting and abusive process, which can become linked with ruminations about the abuse.

# 4

# THERAPY WITH AN OLDER MAN WHO HAD LOST HIS SPEECH

## Introduction

Valerie Sinason has written of long term psychotherapy with a severely handicapped young woman called Maureen who had no speech (Sinason, 1992). It is a marvellous piece which inspired me to undertake the work reported in this chapter. Sinason described her work with Maureen as 'finding meaning without words'. She explained that 'It is precisely the weight of meaning behind every gesture that we can find unbearable' (1992, p. 223). She draws attention to a particular method in working with patients with no speech, little symbolic play or other means of communication: 'It means working far more with the counter-transference feelings and checking them out by the response of the patient. These intuitive responses are clearly honed and deepened by training, (personal) analysis and supervision' (p. 251). Drawing on these skills and sensitivities Sinason worked with a 56 year-old man who was losing his speech as a result of dementia (1992).

It may be recalled that counter-transference refers to all the feelings which are evoked in the therapist through opening him- or herself to the emotional impact of the patient. The patient projects feelings, often of an unbearable nature, into the therapist with the hope that the feelings can be understood and ultimately made bearable – a process which Bion described as containment, beginning in the mother-infant relationship (Chapter 1). The underlying mechanism is projective identification because the recipient of the projections, in this case the therapist, may identify with the projections and experiences the feelings as his or her own. Alternatively the therapist might recognise the unconscious phantasy in the projective identification without becoming identified with the feelings.

However, patients are often acutely sensitive to their therapist's states of mind and can thus mobilise the therapist's feelings, for example feelings such as the therapist's wish to be a good mother to the patient or the therapist's sadism (Brenman Pick, 1985; Young, 1995). The therapist needs to be receptive to the patient's emotional states, and able to reflect on and disentangle personal reactions and transferences to the patient from feelings which the patient may be mobilising which can provide clues to unconscious communication. Sinason has demonstrated how using the counter-transference in this way can help severely handicapped patients feel known and understood. For example she was able to differentiate various emotional meanings expressed by a patient's head banging. Following Sinason's lead I hoped to try to understand and communicate with an older man who could not speak, by thinking and talking about the impact he had on me.

Mr Mitchell was a patient in long stay care and referred to me by the ward's consultant physician because of 'behaviour problems'. I met with the ward sister and some of her staff to discuss the referral. They told me Mr Mitchell was an 80 year-old man who had suffered two strokes. After his first stroke, a few years earlier, he had returned home. He had been looked after by a neighbour or family friend. His wife had died some years previously. When he had a second stroke he lost his speech and the right side of his body was paralysed. He could no longer be managed at home. He had been an in-patient in the hospital for just a few months before he was referred to me. He had two sons, though only one of them visited him. There seemed to be some ill feeling between the sons and between the son who didn't visit and Mr Mitchell. The son who visited each week sometimes brought his two children. Mr Mitchell was obviously delighted to see his grandchildren. There were also occasional visits from the woman friend or neighbour who had looked after him. She told the staff Mr Mitchell had been very kind to her. He had been a bricklayer of exceptional skill. Little more was known about his life.

Mr Mitchell was unable to speak other than to shout obscenities. Still very strong physically, he would occasionally hit out at the staff when they were attending to him. He sometimes shouted throughout the day and into the night, causing uproar on the ward as other patients shouted back. There were mixed views about whether Mr Mitchell could understand what was said to him. Sometimes he appeared to understand and sometimes not. The staff said occasionally he answered 'yes' when they felt he meant 'no', and sometimes 'no' when he meant 'yes'. He was known to be illiterate. The staff appealed to me for help about the shouting and hitting out. A young female nurse who was Mr Mitchell's keyworker was especially troubled. She felt guilty about not wanting to work with Mr Mitchell because he could be so abusive and difficult. She said she did not look forward to seeing him and was aware of leaving him to the end of her duties.

I decided to try to work jointly with Mr Mitchell and his keyworker. I arranged a meeting with them both but the keyworker could not attend, so I saw Mr Mitchell with the ward sister. I had some coloured felt tip pens and paper available in case he might be able to draw something or make some marks to communicate with me. Sister brought him to my office. He was a tall well-built man, towering over his wheelchair. He was almost bald and had no teeth which sometimes gave his face a babyish look. He had a fine aquiline profile and he also reminded me of a venerable ancient Roman. I drew up a chair near him. I said I'd like to know a bit about him. I asked him when he was born. He turned to the sister, laughed and then sobbed inconsolably for most of that time with me. I felt profoundly shocked.

Over the next few months I met with the keyworker alone because I felt reluctant to see Mr Mitchell again. I thought there was little I could achieve because of the difficulties in communicating with him, but essentially I think I was frightened of the pain of his distress. During the time I saw his keyworker I became worried that Mr Mitchell was being physically abused by some of the staff and I have described the work about this in Chapter 8. I saw Mr Mitchell again some months later when he was present at some of the patient and staff meetings I conducted for his ward (Chapter 6 gives a description of similar meetings on another ward). At times he shouted expletives throughout these meetings, so I had some first-hand experience of what the staff complained about.

Fifteen months after my first meeting with Mr Mitchell the staff again asked me for help with him. By then I felt more able to take on this challenge. I offered to see him once a week, arranging to see him for half-hourly sessions in the early evening. I saw him for a total of 29 sessions over the next eight months until he died. I shall now report the therapy as it proceeded over that time.

## Mr Mitchell – who had lost his speech

### Achieving some holding

*Despite Mr Mitchell's incapacity to speak, I searched for meaning in his behaviour in tandem with thinking about my counter-transference. I experienced great discomfort in recognising some of the feelings stirred in me by this work, particularly feelings of hatred and cruelty.*

I established a routine of going to the ward to collect Mr Mitchell and taking him to my office. When I first went to him I would tell him who I was, where we were going and why. I said the staff were worried about his distress. We hoped that meetings with me might help. In my office, which was a short distance from his ward, I positioned his wheelchair alongside and at an angle from where I sat. I did not put the wheelchair brakes on but left them free so if he wished he could move the chair.

Very soon in the first session, using his unparalysed left arm, he wheeled himself away from me until he reached the wall. He began shouting angrily. He had a loud and piercing voice which I found quite frightening. Occasionally he put the brake on the left wheel and then tried to move the wheel, which of course would not budge. Sometimes he groaned and for brief periods he was quiet.

I was worried I would be as speechless as Mr Mitchell. To my relief I found I had some thoughts and was able to share them with him. I talked about how stuck and helpless he felt, perhaps frightened of his rage and consumed with grief. I wondered too if he felt he had put a brake on his life, as though he was responsible for the stroke. After I spoke he sometimes looked at me, as if to ask me what it was I said. I was uncertain if he understood anything.

I took the session to supervision. My supervisor helped me see that Mr Mitchell may have been frightened of me and what I might do to him because it seemed to her he was cowering in fear against the wall. She suggested to me that Mr Mitchell's stroke probably felt like a clamp on him or a strait-jacket and he was locked inside a damaged body, though he was letting me know there was something inside him that he could manoeuvre like the wheelchair. She encouraged me to explain more about the purpose of the therapy to him, remind him of the length of the sessions and that I would be taking him back to the ward. She suggested I look out for any signs from him that he felt what I said was right or wrong.

At the third session he seemed pleased as I arrived to collect him. In my room he stayed longer with me before he backed away to the wall. But he gave out a terrible wail, over and over again, like a child crying for a lost or broken toy. Interspersed with his cries he shouted angrily again. Sometimes in his cries it was as if he was also calling out 'Hallo there' as though trying to catch my attention. Then he seemed very frustrated when he couldn't get through to me. However, there were two or three times when he seemed to agree with what I said. For a brief time it felt like the flow of an ordinary conversation. For example I found myself feeling fed up and when I said I thought he probably felt fed up, he looked interested and seemed to say 'yeh'.

Taking this session to supervision helped me understand more of Mr Mitchell's unrelieved misery: that it was so bad that nothing could make it better. Though he was hoping for some release he was probably also frightened of death which might come with another stroke.

Arriving at the ward for the fourth session I learnt that Mr Mitchell's son had been expected but hadn't turned up. Once in my room Mr Mitchell pulled his chair away to the wall and didn't move back throughout the session. I felt there were only one or two fleeting moments of contact between us in the whole time. As we approached the end of the session, he seemed to get angrier and angrier. On our return to the ward there was no word from his son. I asked for a message to be left for the son to contact me because I thought it could be useful to learn some more about Mr Mitchell's life. His new key-worker told me that she had heard that Mr Mitchell's wife had become an invalid and thereafter he slept in a chair alongside her bed. The son never got in touch with me. He visited less and less.

As I collected Mr Mitchell for the fifth session he started wailing in a way that felt like a complaint. When in my room he gave some really loud yells. I felt worried that anyone overhearing would wonder what on earth I was doing to him. I noticed too that he often shouted over me when I was talking to him. It occurred to me that he was angry with me for being handicapped because he couldn't get through to me. However much he shouted, I couldn't understand what he meant. After a while he pulled his chair away to the wall. He made just one attempt to move back but couldn't because he had put the brake on one of the wheels. I felt tearful. At the same time I was aware of trying to distance myself from him. I talked about his pain and he got angry. I thought he felt I was humiliating him with pity. Later, I found myself thinking about his funeral. I said to him that I thought he wanted to die. He turned to me angrily and shouted very clearly 'No!' I replied that perhaps I hadn't understood his dilemma: he wanted to die but feared dying, and when he wanted to stay alive he feared continuing to live in this condition. He shouted angrily. I said I thought he might be worried about making me angry and that I would retaliate and hurt him in some way.

Towards the end of the session the decibels of Mr Mitchell's shouts escalated. I thought about how horrible it must be for him to now feel like his invalid wife. I remembered the son who had not visited last week and the other son who did not visit at all. I talked about him feeling I was abandoning him at the end of the session, like his loved ones. As I wheeled him out of the room I was shocked to realise I felt angry and cruel towards him.

At the sixth session I found Mr Mitchell in his pyjamas and in bed. His bed was one of 20 in a long corridor ward with beds on either side. A staff member told me Mr Mitchell had been sleepy and 'fighting' with them to go to bed. I pulled up a chair alongside the bed and drew the curtains around the bed for some privacy. He lay with his eyes closed. From time to time his eyes flickered open, just a few times he looked at me. I couldn't tell whether he wanted me to go or stay because he answered 'No' to every question. I decided to stay.

Sitting by his bedside for that half hour was an excruciating experience. I became aware of all the impingements on him: television, radio, staff shouting to each other, relatives and staff conversing and walking back and forth. Just how close the beds were to one another, was forcibly brought home to me when I was elbowed through the curtains by one of the staff attending to an adjacent patient. There was absolutely no privacy. Mr Mitchell lay quietly but once he shouted piercingly at me, giving me quite a shock. I began thinking that in his shouting Mr Mitchell was conveying some of his experience on the ward of having so much intrude into him, day in and day out.

When he became quiet I felt I was at the bedside of a dying man. I thought he might feel frightened of going to sleep in case he would not wake up, but I was unable to voice such a thought there on the ward.

At the eighth session, just three weeks to go before my summer holiday, Mr Mitchell's shirt was stained with food and he was unshaven. His shouts were especially piercing and frightening. I wondered if that was what the stroke felt like. I told Mr Mitchell about my holiday, how many weeks to go, how long I'd be away and when I would be back. He pulled his chair away. He was quiet as he sat against the wall. He looked in the distance as if having a thought or a memory and then he cried out again. I said that when I was able to think about his pain then he seemed able to hold a thought in mind, but that brought another pain: for a moment he was somewhere else, sometime else and then he was back with the inconsolable grief of being here in hospital.

Just before the end of the session one of his slippers fell off. I asked him if he wanted me to put it back on. I thought he said yes. I put it back on his foot and as I prepared to wheel him back to the ward he held out his hand to me. I shook it. I felt very touched. When we entered the ward a nursing auxiliary, who was a temp from an agency, shouted at Mr Mitchell 'Do you want to go to bed?' and then 'Are you wet?' I felt most uncomfortable leaving him.

When I entered the ward for the ninth session, the senior nurse told me in a sympathetic way that Mr Mitchell had a cold and was feeling miserable. I noticed his clothes because he was wearing a nice cardigan and a clean shirt. In my room, for the first time, he didn't pull his chair away but stayed sitting near me. He was quiet and appeared to be a bit drowsy but his eyes remained open. Occasionally he made some soft sounds as if to tell me he was still awake. Sometimes I thought he looked contemplative. Being with him felt peaceful. I wondered aloud if he felt sad and he seemed to say 'Aye?', so I repeated what I said. He seemed to agree. At one point he cried out, it seemed in anguish. I said it was painful to think, to remember and to be aware of where he is; and sad to think of what he has lost and that he will be losing me who gives him a hand, losing me during my holiday. Again he seemed to agree. As the end of the session drew near he became noisier. I talked about him feeling upset as we got near the end of the session and nearer to the holiday. He was quiet again as we returned to the ward.

## Commentary

When I started working with Mr Mitchell it was shocking to find I could feel cruel towards this vulnerable old man, just as I also found it difficult to see that he could feel frightened of me. I was soon drawn into cruel exchanges with him when I made interpretations about him wanting to die which enraged him. There may be truth in these interpretations but I think they also conveyed my hatred of being with Mr Mitchell and my wish he would die. This experience was a salutary lesson about how troubling it must be for care staff to experience hateful feelings when working with patients like Mr Mitchell. His sometimes dishevelled, food-stained state was doubtless a reflection of his aggressiveness, which obstructed staff from cleaning him and of problems of staff shortages on the ward, but it probably also reflected conscious or unconscious retaliation.

I began to understand how Mr Mitchell could provoke abusive treatment. Such provocations may have been a reaction to the trauma of his strokes in which he drew abuse onto himself 'as a way of controlling the disturbance ... to repeat the trauma in an assimilable experience and to omnipotently compensate for his handicap' (Sinason writing about one of her handicapped patients, 1986, p. 150). The provocations may also have been a result of abuse on the ward (and/or even earlier abuse in his life) as a result of him identifying with the aggressor 'as a means of psychic survival' (Milton, 1994).

Supervision was very important in helping me to think, especially because in some respects I felt I became somewhat handicapped and unable to think in the sessions. I came to realise that from Mr Mitchell's point of view I could appear frustratingly disabled because I could not understand him. It was undoubtedly painful to try to put myself in his shoes, but I may have become unconsciously identified with his handicapped condition perhaps to avoid thinking. Having another perspective from supervision helped me disentangle myself from him.

In the fourth session I did not see the obvious connection between his son failing to visit him that day and his withdrawal during the session. It took me another week to bear the pain of recognising his feelings of abandonment. Mr Mitchell's family may not have visited or visited infrequently because of their feelings about seeing him reduced to such a dreadful condition. Nonetheless as Peter Hildebrand has pointed out 'The intervention of the state has not helped here, since for so many the fact that it will supply an old people's home for their dependent relatives offers them the chance to avoid the working through of their feelings and attitudes to their parents in their later years' (1995, p. 93). My own intervention of weekly sessions with Mr Mitchell may have contributed to his family's withdrawal because they felt less need to visit.

The sessions leading up to the holiday illustrate developments that can be achieved in work of this kind. Being at Mr Mitchell's bedside helped me understand more about the constant impingements he endured on the ward and how his shouting may have conveyed something of that experience. My staying alongside his bed must have meant a lot to him because the following week, the seventh session, he stayed longer sitting by me before retreating to the wall and there was more of a conversational flow. The next session he appeared more able to hold a thought in his mind because I think he felt more held by me. The experience of simply trying to think about someone and resisting the urge to do anything, is comparable to the maternal holding that Esther Bick (1968) saw as so important for the infant, because it can enable an older patient like Mr Mitchell to feel that what may be fragmented and chaotic experiences can be gathered together and held in another person's mind.

The episode of the dropped slipper indicates the value, for patients and carers, of looking for meaning in tiny pieces of behaviour which might otherwise go unnoticed or be dismissed as irrelevant or mere chance. Mr Mitchell's slipper had not fallen off before and its falling off followed the news of my holiday. Nor had Mr Mitchell held his hand out to me before. The slipper offered a metaphor for a feeling of being dropped by me during the holiday. Holding out his hand as well as expressing his gratitude could also have been a way of letting me know he felt held. The next week he showed a connectedness to me when he did not move his chair away but sat by me throughout the session; not only did he look better dressed and cared for but the nurse seemed more sympathetic towards him. Sinason has written 'Understanding or trying to understand meaning does not necessarily make disturbance or aggressive behaviour go away, but it can lessen the extent of the damage to our clients and make us and our colleagues feel more able to bear the difficulties' (1992, p. 227).

## Establishing a vocabulary

*Mr Mitchell became more settled for a while. He continued to reach out for contact. However, as the Christmas break approached his anger escalated and there was some retaliatory behaviour from his carers.*

After I returned from holiday when I went to collect Mr Mitchell his clothes were stained with food. There was food still on his face and smeared over his wheelchair. One of the auxiliaries wiped his face. I said we were going to my room. He shouted 'No!' and kept shouting as I wheeled him down the corridor. Perhaps this shouting was a protest about my absence over the holiday, it was hard to know. In the room he put the brake on his chair and stayed near me. For a while there was a feeling of a conversational flow between his noises and my talk. A couple of times he seemed to be trying to mouth some words. I couldn't understand him. Then he began wailing in an inconsolable way. I said 'You are sad today' and he replied very clearly 'Yes'. He became quiet and almost fell asleep.

A cat cried outside my window, wanting to get in. Mr Mitchell stirred. I said I thought he felt excluded and forgotten like the cat during my holiday. Perhaps he thought I might forget him again when the session ended. He was quiet for a while and then began wailing. I talked about what I thought he had lost in his life, his sadness and the pain. For a moment he looked searchingly into my eyes. Later, as we entered the ward he called out 'No!' At that moment I too hated the ward. An auxiliary came up to us, greeting Mr Mitchell in a loud and cheerful voice. A senior staff member called me over to tell me Mr Mitchell had been 'up and down'.

At the sixteenth session the nurse who greeted me spoke warmly about Mr Mitchell but also complained of having worked for eight days without a break. In the session there was little contact with Mr Mitchell. I felt I must be mad to think he understood anything I was saying, or got anything from the sessions. There was just no way of knowing. I kept looking at the clock, longing for the end of the session.

I talked to him about time hanging heavily and then about him wanting to die. For a moment he looked at me angrily. I thought 'so he has understood something I've said'. I then said, more kindly, that he was probably frightened of dying. He wiped his brow. I thought it must be such an effort for him to keep on going.

Later, my supervisor helped me think about what felt unbearable: Mr Mitchell's fear and terror and his existence which gets worse and worse, perhaps especially the not-knowing-how-long-it-will-go-on-for. He wanted me to know how it feels. He was dealing with something that was driving him crazy. What do you do when your internal situation is intolerable and when you try to externalise it by putting it into others so they might understand, they too find it intolerable? How could I take him back to the ward after being with me in my quiet room: is it that I don't know what the ward is like or am I cruel?

In the seventeenth session he was quiet. He seemed extremely sad. I found my thoughts wandering away. I talked to him about how I thought he felt that I could not bear to stay with his pain. He almost drifted off to sleep. Unusually I too felt sleepy. Occasionally he cried out as though he appeared to become aware of where he was, waking with a jolt into a living nightmare.

I noticed he moved his good arm as if to reach out to me. I was unsure whether to take his hand or not. Perhaps he was simply adjusting his position. It seemed different from before. I talked about him wanting to reach out to me and be held when he felt lonely. At the nineteenth session he again started moving his arm towards me, then putting it back on his lap or on the arm rest of his chair. I decided to take hold of his hand. He held my hand for a moment, as if wanting to pull me towards him, and then he let it go. This happened several times. I said holding my hand was a bit of contact. He said 'Yeh', very clearly. After the halfway time in the session he abruptly pulled his chair away to the wall, something he had not done for some weeks. He started angrily shouting. I said it's hard getting close and then I drop him when I take him back to the ward. He seemed to agree but I was uncertain. I began feeling I didn't understand anything as Mr Mitchell became angrier all the while.

In supervision I talked about how hard it was to know if anything I said to Mr Mitchell was right. My supervisor suggested Mr Mitchell was leaving me in the dark perhaps because he felt I didn't need to be told or he might have been showing me how in the dark he felt. She said it was probably hard for him to keep in contact with me. She pointed out the vocabulary he and I were establishing through his different moods and gestures. I felt encouraged.

At the twenty-second session, just four weeks until my Christmas break, the ward sister told me Mr Mitchell had been very noisy during the day. Somewhat apologetically she said he should have been changed, meaning a soiled pad should have been removed. I said it must be uncomfortable for him. She replied that she doubted he could tell the difference but it would be unpleasant for me. There was food spilled over his clothing and a smell of faecal incontinence. In my room he rocked himself back and forth in his chair, pulling himself upright then falling back, crossing and uncrossing his good leg over his paralysed one. He alternately shouted and groaned. I said I thought he was angry about being treated like a naughty baby and left in soiled nappy. He didn't seem to react. After one very loud shout I thought he was about to weep. I was reminded of the first time I met him when he sobbed in my room.

I told Mr Mitchell about the Christmas holiday. He seemed to get angrier and kept looking away, ignoring whatever I said. Later, with just a few minutes left in the session he pushed his chair away. I noticed he used his good foot to propel his chair, whereas formerly he had used his arm. By the end of the session I was reeling from the smell in the room.

When I arrived to collect Mr Mitchell for the twenty-sixth session, the last before the Christmas holiday, the ward sister looked relieved to see me. She said Mr Mitchell had been very noisy all day. As I took him out of the ward one of the other patients muttered angrily about him. Mr Mitchell was unshaven but wearing a pleasantly patterned pullover. He shouted as we entered the room but did not move his chair away from me. I said I thought he was upset about the coming holiday. He became calm, making gentle sounds and sometimes looking drowsy. At one point he moved his hand towards me. I took it and held it for a moment until he let it drop. He looked over at me from time to time and occasionally nodded off.

At the end of the session he put his foot on the floor. I could not move his chair. I said he didn't want to leave. He kept his foot on the floor. I felt perplexed. I asked if he wanted his foot put on the foot rest of the chair. He didn't respond but I put his foot on the footrest and took him back to the ward. The ward sister was surprised to see Mr Mitchell so quiet. I explained that he was upset about the holiday. She seemed interested by this explanation.

## Commentary

This work with Mr Mitchell helped him be more in touch with his misery and his depressive feelings and less tormented. But I can now see that as Mr Mitchell became sadder I found it hard to bear his grief and at times my interpretations took him and me away from sad feelings. It was especially difficult seeing the comfort he felt from being with me and then his distress as we approached the end of the sessions. I felt very guilty about taking him back to the ward. However, at times when I made the link between approaching the end of the sessions and his increasing upset, it seemed to help him and me bear the feelings. What was brought home to me was the anguish of helping someone like Mr Mitchell stay in touch with sad and sorrowful feelings. Sometimes it was as though feeling persecuted by his shouting was preferable for him and me.

Supervision was crucial in enabling me to stay with the work, to process some of my own difficult emotions and particularly to feel that my distress was being held and understood. I was helped to keep in mind that some of my tormented feelings were possibly also a communication of Mr Mitchell's torment. I was able to appreciate the achievements in the work which I think is often a problem for these older people: how to stay in touch with their achievements in the face of the devastation of physical and mental decline.

The session in which Mr Mitchell had been left so long in a soiled pad shows how cruelty can be inflicted by unthinking behaviour. It is likely that this was in retaliation for his shouting and aggressiveness. Nursing and care staff are vulnerable to acting out negative feelings because it is usually regarded as unacceptable for them to admit to such feelings towards their patients. Peter Speck has described the 'chronic niceness' which can burden staff in a hospice (1994); and Vega Zagier Roberts has explained 'In all caring work there are elements of uncaring' and the caring task 'at times can be hateful ... Obsessional routines of care can serve to protect patients from carers' unconscious hate, from what staff fear they might do to those in their charge if not controlled by rigid discipline. At the same time these routines can provide organisationally sanctioned ways of expressing hate of patients who exhaust, disgust or disappoint staff' (1994, p. 83). Drawing on the work of Winnicott, Zagier Roberts makes the crucial observation that the capacity to tolerate hatred without enacting it depends on being 'thoroughly aware of one's hate' (1994, p. 83). To achieve this kind of awareness care staff need training programmes and support structures which permit them to acknowledge uncaring feelings. In Chapter 8 I describe how providing therapeutic consultations for staff can help them challenge and prevent abusive practices.

The news of the second holiday shows further evidence of Mr Mitchell's understanding and how he could expand his range of expressiveness. This time he literally put his foot down about the holiday. The reports of Mr Mitchell's anger on the ward suggest that some of the anger stirred by the holiday was being expressed on the ward. Perhaps I could have done more to link the anger with myself and gather it into the transference to try to ease the situation on the ward. Alternatively, it may be that at this juncture of his life, Mr Mitchell could only manage by this kind of splitting in order to preserve something good in the sessions and inside himself.

The conversation with the ward sister when she showed interest in the connection I made between Mr Mitchell's aggressiveness and my holiday makes me aware of how relatively little contact I had with the staff on Mr Mitchell's ward. I could see that the staff were appreciative of the interest I showed in Mr Mitchell but I perpetuated an unhelpful distance between the staff and myself. Regular discussions with the staff about my work with Mr Mitchell would have been a way of supporting the work and the staff.

## Mourning and letting go

*After this second holiday Mr Mitchell withdrew from contact. The final two sessions were at his bedside on the ward before he died. On the ward I found it hard to give expression to some of my thoughts about him dying. It was difficult too to simply be with him without intruding as he took his farewell.*

On my return from the Christmas break I found Mr Mitchell asleep in his chair. He woke as I approached him but I couldn't tell if he recognised me. His foot was again on the floor. I could only see two agency staff whom I didn't know. Once in my room he slept until the last ten minutes of the session. When he woke he rocked himself forward several times. I said I thought he was uncomfortable in the chair. He replied clearly 'Yeh'. I said that perhaps he was tired and fed up with me because of the holiday. He seemed to stir. I talked of time hanging very heavily. I wondered if he had felt he might not see me again. Perhaps he thought he was dreaming when he first saw me today.

Just a few minutes before the end of the session he became agitated. I spoke of his awareness that there wasn't much time left, now in the session or in his life. He pushed his chair away with his foot in a defiant manner. As I tried to wheel him out of the room he put his foot down and stopped the chair. I said he was putting his foot down about not wanting to leave. He lifted his foot and I took him back. He gave some quiet groans as we entered the ward.

At the twenty-eighth session one of the nurses told me Mr Mitchell was ill and had been refusing food. He wouldn't even eat his porridge which was unusual for him and he had been quiet, not his usual self. She told me another patient had died the previous night after having a fit. I sat by Mr Mitchell's bed with the curtains drawn around us. He was lying on his back, his mouth open and his eyes half closed. I noticed his very wrinkled neck. He was quiet. A nearby television intruded into my thoughts. I heard an older actor being interviewed about her tips for keeping young, and later some news about NHS closures and hospitals fighting to survive.

Mr Mitchell called out, at first somewhat quietly and then louder, as if to pull me back to him and remind me there was still some life in him. He became quiet again. I thought he was pleased I was there. I then worried he might die at any moment. I watched to see if he was still breathing. He stirred occasionally. I thought he was showing me he was still alive. I talked about him feeling frightened of dying and uncomfortable to be alive, a terrible dilemma. He did not seem to react.

Sometimes he turned his head to look at me, I thought to see if I was still there or, perhaps, if he was. Sometimes he sounded angry. I wondered if he was angry to be still alive or angry to be giving up and dying. I thought he might feel I would be glad if he died but I felt that was a thought I couldn't voice in public on the ward. I thought he might be angry too about the constant intrusion of the television. There was no peace there.

Suddenly one of the nurses pulled the curtains open and then apologised when she saw me there. Perhaps she thought the curtains around the bed meant that Mr Mitchell had died. She told me, in whispers, there had been another death on the ward and Mr Mitchell had not been well. Mr Mitchell looked as if he was dosing off though he stayed awake. I said good-bye and that I would see him next week.

At the twenty-ninth session Mr Mitchell lay in his bed, his head propped up high on pillows. The senior nurse was giving Mr Mitchell something to drink from a beaker. She explained she wanted to get something inside him. I pulled the curtains around the bed. I noticed traces of food on the sheets. Mr Mitchell's eyes were just partly open. There was some sticky secretion around his eyelids. His mouth was open and I could hear him breathing heavily. I thought of the phrase 'the breath of life'. It seemed hard for him to hold on and hard to let go, an enormous effort.

He kept moving his arm or leg, sometimes his lip, again I thought to let me know he was still alive. Just occasionally he turned to look at me. Then, in the latter half of the session he did not look at me at all.

He gave a few soft groans. That was all. Once more I wondered if he felt I was impatient for him to die but I could not say it. Amidst the usual noise of the ward I overheard an agency nurse auxiliary joking. Later he abruptly pulled the curtains aside and then apologised. I had been told that Mr Mitchell's family were informed of his condition. Only the one son visited. When I said good-bye Mr Mitchell looked angrily at me and closed his eyes.

Five days later Mr Mitchell died. One of his sons was with him. The other son phoned the next day to complain to the staff that he had not been told. Both sons said they did not want any of Mr Mitchell's clothes or possessions from the ward. When I went to the ward, the sister and Mr Mitchell's keyworker were packing Mr Mitchell's belongings. The sister told me the sons didn't even want the nice framed photograph of Mr Mitchell's grandchildren. I watched her sadly taking Mr Mitchell's name label off his shaver and packing it to send to a charity. Mr Mitchell's keyworker was tearful. She said another patient who used to get angry with Mr Mitchell was very upset about his death.

I felt a mixture of relief and sadness. I was relieved for him and about not having to see him again, but also I missed him.

## Commentary

I think my reluctance to voice some of my thoughts about dying when I was at Mr Mitchell's bedside reflects some of the pressure against thinking or speaking about such topics on the wards. Though death was a common experience it was nonetheless a difficult subject for staff to discuss. One of the nurses alluded to her awareness of Mr Mitchell dying when she told me of another patient who had died, but she did not speak about it explicitly.

I think the outcome of the therapy with Mr Mitchell was that he was enabled to face his death, let go of life and die. The two holiday breaks helped me focus the grieving work. Mr Mitchell could not speak and it was not possible to be sure about how he experienced loss. However, having established a link with him I was then able to help him mourn my loss and implicitly other losses revived for him in the transference. When I could bear the pain of his sad, depressive feelings and he felt held by me, he could begin to let go. Reaching his hand out to me, letting me hold it then dropping it, conveyed this process of feeling held and letting go. His sleepiness in these later sessions and my corresponding drowsiness seemed an indication of him beginning to withdraw from attachments. Hence the therapy had perhaps facilitated a process of 'anticipatory mourning' for the end of his life, as also discussed in relation to therapy with Mrs Taylor 'who collapsed into helplessness' in Chapter 3.

In the last weeks of his life, Mr Mitchell's refusal to eat seemed an active expression of his wish to die, a phenomenon I had by then become familiar with in these older patients. I heard of other patients in long stay care who reached a point where they refused to eat or drink, clearly signalling their intention to die. The final sessions at Mr Mitchell's bedside show the difficulty of trying to stay in contact with him and at the same time allowing him to withdraw. When I offered interpretations I think I was being intrusive. Essentially the task became to allow Mr Mitchell to take his leave of me and die which meant being with him in a way that required nothing of him.

In a discussion with my supervisor about the final sessions, she commented on the nurses' valuable skill in recognising when a patient is dying, a skill that often goes unacknowledged and unappreciated. The way the nursing and care staff were left to deal with Mr Mitchell's death is unfortunately typical of the way responsibility for the old and dying are relegated to these staff by a society that finds death intolerable.

Finally, I have been asked why I chose to work with Mr Mitchell who could not speak. On reflection, I think I felt identified with his inability to express himself, an aspect of myself which I became aware of in my own therapy. I realise how invaluable it was to have someone there for me, endeavouring to find words for what I could not say.

## Summary

Working with the consequences of severe disability such as the aftermath of Mr Mitchell's stroke which left him paralysed and without speech, means finding alternative ways of making contact. Having someone trying to think about and make sense of experiences for which there are no longer words can help these patients feel held. A vocabulary may be discovered though close observation of minute detail of gestures and other behaviour and by reflecting on the countertransference. Disabled patients who understandably may be angry and frustrated can provoke negative feelings such as hatred and cruelty. It is important therapists or carers have opportunities for reflection, with a supervisor or other colleagues, to help process these feelings so that they are not enacted, and to make bearable distressing and tormenting states of mind, particularly by understanding that such states may be evoked by patients as a way of trying to convey something of their own internal struggle.

Achieving some emotional closeness through therapy can provide an opportunity to address issues of grief and bereavement, and help patients mourn the damage wrought by disability and face their deaths. Closeness and intimacy come from recognition of separateness and loss especially by working through the feelings stirred by partings in the therapy. In working with very ill and disabled older people it can be particularly difficult to bear the pain of the patient's grief, to relinquish the therapeutic ties and allow the patient to die.

# 5

# OLDER COUPLES

## Introduction

Psychoanalytically oriented therapy with couples identifies two fundamental needs in a couple's relationship: the need for intimacy and the need to be separate, with their attendant anxieties of either being swallowed up or abandoned (Ruszczynski, 1993). These anxieties resonate with our earliest experience of being part of a couple in the infant and mother relationship. The capacity to develop and sustain a couple relationship depends on how we negotiated that first attachment in the context of the triangular constellation known as the 'Oedipus complex'. The Oedipus complex, essentially unconscious, was first outlined by Freud and refers to the infant's and child's passionate attachment to a parent of the opposite sex, and rivalry with the same sex parent. Particularly as developed by Klein the Oedipus complex is understood to include a negative or inverted complex involving a passionate attachment to the same sex parent and rivalry with the opposite sex parent. ('Parent' needs to be understood as referring to the primary carers.) James Fisher describes the nature of these erotic Oedipal attachments as 'painfully tragic' because they reach 'across a chasm, a chasm created by the inexorable difference between the generations, by the reality of the difference of the experience of being the parent and the experience of being the child' (1993, p. 150). Ron Britton (1989) in an important paper about the Oedipus complex develops further the understanding of the very difficult tasks faced by the infant or child because he or she has to manage both being in a close relationship to mother, (or primary carer), which excludes another, (father or other third figure), and at the same time has a growing awareness of a special, usually sexual, couple relationship from which the infant or child is excluded.

In essence, working through this Oedipal dilemma means working through 'depressive anxieties' which arise from the realisation of feelings of love and hate for the same person and the awareness that there are others with whom the loved one is involved. How well this is managed will depend on internal factors, like envy and externally on how the child's carers manage the inclusion and exclusion, and the kind of model of a couple which they provide and which can be internalised. Where the infant or child experiences a poor early relationship, either between the parental couple, or between him- or herself and the parents, later as an adult he or she may look to his or her own coupling to make up for what was missed, and the couple relationship may be idealised. If found lacking the couple relationship may then be denigrated because of the difficulty of bearing disappointment.

Therapy with a couple means monitoring, though not necessarily interpreting, their individual transferences to the therapist and to one another. Whether the therapist works in a pair with another therapist, or singly as in the work I describe in this chapter, it is important to keep in mind the transference onto the therapist(s) as a couple: the couple transference refers to the unconscious view of the relationship, or to put this another way, the projections into the couple relationship. The relationship between two therapists working together presents a receptacle for such projections; but so too the single therapist, for example when the single therapist's interpretations may be experienced as a product of an internal creative coupling or dialogue.

The couple transference onto the therapist(s) is of crucial significance in this work because it offers a way of understanding the unconscious meaning of the couple's relationship and what is projected into it. Stanley Ruszczynski (1993) describes how a partner is selected, unconsciously, as a suitable receptacle for projective identification to contain parts of oneself, *defensively* because these aspects cannot be tolerated, and *with the developmental hope* that at some time it may be possible to integrate these parts within oneself. Fisher (1995) distinguishes this use of projective identification from an 'intrusive' projective identification used in phantasy to get inside the other and establish a 'pseudo intimacy', which denies separateness and brings a certainty about knowing the other person; whereas 'mature intimacy' means tolerating the 'infinitely unknowable mystery of the reality of the other'. Drawing on Keats and Bion, Fisher writes that whatever intimate knowledge of the other, there are always 'uncertainties, mysteries and doubts' (p. 104).

If all goes well the couple relationship operates as a creative container in which the tensions and conflicts between the couple can be worked through. Warren Colman writes that the couple relationship 'does not have to be the place where I can entirely be myself, but it can be the place where I discover some of the possibilities for becoming myself' (1993, p. 141). Colman differentiates this notion of creative containment from 'defensive containment' for a couple where one partner offers containment to the other, as a mother does for her infant.

Sandra Evans (2004a) has described developments in therapy for older couples, including group therapy. For the older couple particular difficulties may arise from the consequences of children leaving home, retirement, and the effects of ageing, illness and disability. A pressing tension in the older couple relationship is the ever encroaching reality of one's own and one's partner's death and the end of the relationship. In the following studies of the couples with whom I worked, whatever the grievances and disappointments about the relationships, I think they were all struggling with the anticipation of this final loss.

## Some problems engaging older couples in therapy

### Mrs Henderson – for whom retirement became a nightmare

*Mrs Henderson split off and evacuated her grief and despair into her husband, and into myself. Her reluctance to invite her husband to join her in the sessions suggests a fear of examining the marital relationship and retrieving the feelings she had projected into her husband. Perhaps my difficulty in continuing to work with her alone reflected my intolerance of her projected feelings.*

A woman in her early seventies, Mrs Henderson was referred to me by her GP because she suffered from panic attacks and claustrophobia which had only occurred in the last few years. Mrs Henderson was a quiet-spoken woman and was well-groomed with an air of refinement, giving the impression of a faded gentility. She spent most of the first assessment meeting complaining about her husband. Since his retirement, several years earlier, he had been angry, unpredictable and would fly into rages against her. He was furious about the retirement settlement from his job because when he retired he was given no pension, only a new car. Now their life was very restricted owing to reduced finances. Recently he had locked her in their dining room whilst she was making a weekly phone call to a friend. She felt he was jealous of her talking to her friend. Since he was at home all the time he rarely let her out of his sight. She said he often experienced a shortness of breath and was worried about dying.

Mrs Henderson mentioned she suffered from nightmares. I asked her if she could tell me any that she remembered. She described a dream in which she got into a panic about not being able to find her way home from a particular seaside resort. I asked her about her thoughts about the dream. She said she and her husband had regularly stayed at this resort until his retirement when they could no longer afford to go back. They had since argued about whether they might try some cheaper form of holiday. She then described another dream in which she became very frightened because someone was trying to put a veil over her head. She had no associations to this second dream.

Towards the conclusion of this first meeting, I said I thought Mrs Henderson might also be feeling angry since her husband's retirement and the claustrophobic existence they now lived. She too might be feeling her age and frightened of dying. Mrs Henderson looked puzzled. She said she felt the problem was her husband and his unreasonable behaviour. I said I thought it could be helpful to see her with her husband. She quickly replied he would go mad if she suggested such a thing. He would not admit he had a problem nor be willing to see anybody about it. I concluded this meeting by offering her a further appointment. Again I suggested she try to talk it over with her husband and ask him to accompany her to the next appointment.

When I saw Mrs Henderson a fortnight later, she came alone and spoke in much the same way as on the first meeting, complaining about her husband's anger and the miserable life with him. She was again reluctant to consider that she shared any of her husband's feelings, or to ask him to join us in further meetings. I felt despair. I said I thought the difficulties resided in their relationship and needed to be addressed in joint meetings, but if she changed her mind about including her husband then I would be happy to see them both in the future. Some weeks later I had a polite note from Mrs Henderson in which she thanked me for seeing her.

*Commentary*

Mrs Henderson is an example of a client coming for therapy but presenting someone else, in this case her husband, as the problem. In such cases it can be useful to think about whether the client is also describing problematic aspects of him- or herself and to listen to the client's account as possibly about an intra-personal difficulty, not just an interpersonal one. In other words this may be a projective process in which one member of the couple projects unmanageable feelings into the partner. Projective identification often has an effect on the recipient and may find resonance with and hook into feelings in the recipient. Thus Mr Henderson's difficult behaviour may have reflected his own and his wife's feelings.

Mrs Henderson's dreams support a hypothesis of a projective process in which her husband was carrying unwanted feelings on her behalf. The nightmares reveal Mrs Henderson's fear of her angry feelings about their reduced circumstances, and of her worries about dying. To interpret the dreams it was useful to think of all the material in the session as possible associations as well as to elicit specific associations from the client. Otherwise there is a danger of making erroneous interpretations based only on the therapist's associations. Although Mrs Henderson did not produce associations for the second dream, the image of a veil being put over her head suggests some of the classical depictions of death, indicated by a veil or a shroud placed over a corpse. This image resonated with her talk of her husband's fears of death. I think Mrs Henderson was too frightened to consider some of these feelings within herself; and was therefore unable to co-operate in couple therapy in which the splitting and projection between her and her husband could be addressed. I felt that Mrs Henderson evacuated some of her disappointment and frustration into me, a reason perhaps for her polite thanks. There was little reflection or movement between the two meetings which did not augur well for continuing to see Mrs Henderson individually. However, I may have acted out some of the projected frustration and hopelessness by not offering to try some individual therapy.

Whilst the reduction in this couple's circumstances might have been weathered more easily earlier in their lives, it had a particularly difficult meaning at this later stage because it doubtless galvanised around other losses they were experiencing, like the grief about retirement, the loss of physical capacities and the anticipation of death. The loss of work can be particularly problematic because aspects of work like its structure, content, routine, security and esteem, provide an important means of managing profound anxieties. Retirement which usually follows the children leaving home means that the couple are often living much more in each other's pockets than ever before. Thus retirement can place a great deal of strain on the couple relationship.

### Mr and Mrs Johnson – a couple betrayed and tormented by illness

*I was drawn into a tormenting struggle between this couple, in which it seemed old scores about sexual jealousy were now being settled as the previously 'live wire' Mrs Johnson became incapacitated. In the transference I too experienced a betrayal, especially in the way they concluded the therapy.*

Mrs Johnson, a 64 year-old woman, suffered from Parkinson's Disease and had spent two weeks on the rehabilitation ward. Shortly before she was discharged she was referred by the consultant physician who was concerned about Mr Johnson being too protective of his wife. Mr Johnson complained that his wife used to hallucinate, though none of the staff on the ward had seen any evidence of it. Kay, a nurse auxiliary was Mrs Johnson's keyworker (or 'named nurse'). She felt Mrs Johnson had lost a lot of self-respect and confidence since the onset of the Parkinson's Disease, particularly because Mr Johnson now treated his wife like a child. Kay had taken her out shopping. They had bought some make-up which Mrs Johnson was now using. I asked Kay if she would be interested in joining me in some sessions with Mr and Mrs Johnson. She seemed pleased to take part, but as it happened she only attended two of the meetings because of difficulty getting away from the ward or changes in her shift.

Mrs Johnson was a slight woman, just reaching up to her husband's shoulder. She leaned on his arm as she came into the room, walking hesitantly in small steps. Her speech was sometimes difficult to understand because she spoke quickly with all the words getting jumbled up. Sometimes her husband would act as interpreter for her speech. At times even he could not understand her and, with obvious irritation, he would ask her to repeat what she said.

I saw them fortnightly for one-hour sessions, over a period of five months. Each time they came, Mr Johnson would begin by complaining about his wife's hallucinations. Mrs Johnson would listen impassively as though her husband was talking about someone else. Once I met their son visiting on the ward. He confirmed that his mother did hallucinate, mostly seeing himself and his brother when they were small. However, Mrs Johnson's husband said she also used to say another man was poking her on the sofa, or she would accuse Mr Johnson of being unfaithful. The hallucinations made Mr Johnson extremely angry and he would appeal to me to rid his wife of them. I thought the hallucinations were a distraction from the grief about Mrs Johnson's illness and increasing disability, but I felt under pressure to make sense of the content of the hallucinations.

As the history of Mrs Johnson's illness emerged, it was clear it had dealt a dreadful blow to their plans for retirement. Mr Johnson had to retire several months early in order to take care of his wife. They had planned to move to a bungalow by the sea but now felt this was impossible because of Mrs Johnson's condition. During the time I saw them she began to experience increasing difficulty climbing the stairs at home. More and more Mr Johnson felt she could not be left alone. When his wife had become ill, Mr Johnson's three brothers all died within a short space of time. I felt he was still shocked and grieving these deaths and his wife's illness. Although he looked tearful when I said this, he could not admit to feeling sad. Instead he started to talk again about his wife's hallucinations.

It seemed Mr and Mrs Johnson's relationship had probably been an unhappy one for some time before her illness. On one occasion, with some bitterness in his voice, Mr Johnson described his wife as always being aloof and inaccessible, just as she often appeared in the sessions. They were quite isolated with few friends. One son lived abroad and they rarely saw him. The other son, though living nearby, visited infrequently. I had the impression that they had lived a lonely life for some time, though Mr Johnson complained that they were isolated because his wife refused to go out for fear of people seeing her in a disabled state.

From the beginning there was a sexual theme in the material, whether about making Mrs Johnson more attractive with make-up, the hallucinations about a man poking her, or her accusations that her husband was unfaithful. When I took up this theme they admitted their sexual relationship had ceased some years before. Mrs Johnson looked hurt as we discussed sex. She implied that she felt sex had stopped for no good reason. Mr Johnson was clearly embarrassed. He talked about how awkward he felt about becoming a nurse for his wife by looking after her in such intimate ways as bathing her and assisting her in the toilet. They were unused to such physical intimacy and would never previously have gone into the bathroom together.

Several weeks after I started seeing them, they went out to a social club, the first time for many months. They were clearly pleased to tell me about this excursion. Then Mr Johnson described in great detail the embarrassment about taking his wife to the toilet during the evening. I wondered why he had made such a business of it, asking the other women present not to use the toilet whilst he was in there with his wife. I thought he could have asked another woman to take his wife. I felt the evening had probably been painful because it would have reminded them of earlier times they had enjoyed together before Mrs Johnson became ill. They were confronted with how disabled she had become, no longer the 'live wire' dancer she once was. But instead of this pain they became embroiled in an argument about Mr Johnson taking her to the toilet.

The hallucinations remained a recurring issue, which I began to find irritating. It was possible the hallucinations were a side-effect of the medication for the treatment of the Parkinson's Disease. Some alterations had been made in the medication with little noticeable effect. However, Mr Johnson persisted questioning me about the possible biochemical origin of these symptoms. I admitted the possibility but reminded him that the medics had referred his wife because they were puzzled. Moreover, it was probably a complex interaction between the physical and emotional consequences of the illness. I spoke about noticing that whenever Mrs Johnson or her husband began expressing some of their sad feelings, the other one would start talking about the hallucinations. When there was evidence that Mrs Johnson's Parkinson's Disease was worsening, they again became preoccupied with the hallucinations.

On three occasions during the time I saw them, they consulted doctors about the hallucinations, each time without warning me. They came back after the consultations in a triumphant attitude, telling me they had been reassured the hallucinations were biochemical in origin. On the final occasion they said they would prefer to continue seeing the doctor who had given them such helpful advice. I agreed that it would be confusing to continue seeing myself and the doctor at the same time, but said if they wanted to pursue therapy I would see them again. They did not return.

## Commentary

Therapy with Mr and Mrs Johnson was hindered by a strong negative transference including envy and jealousy which I failed to address sufficiently. To some extent I became disabled and unable to think about their envious attacks on myself who was able-bodied, relatively young and employed. It could have been useful to talk to Mr and Mrs Johnson about how they experienced me (in the transference) as a disabled therapist who was hallucinating useless interpretations about their inner worlds in contrast to the helpful doctors who gave them physical explanations and reassurance; or perhaps their discomfort about revealing intimate aspects of their lives in front of a stranger, like the discomfort about the toilet they experienced at the social club. The negative transference was especially important because it reflected a disparaged view of their marriage, a view which probably had a long history and which was exacerbated by Mrs Johnson's illness. The sexual jealousy and envy which emerged in the sessions hooked into a lifetime's quarrel with each other.

Their individual transferences to each other were also enacted in the therapy with me: Mr Johnson took over so many of his wife's jobs making her retired like he had been, and eventually he made me redundant. Mrs Johnson tormented her husband with the hallucinations so that he thought he might lose his mind, just as she feared she might become a 'cabbage'. I too began to find the hallucinations tormenting, interfering with my capacity to think about what was going on. They also passed onto me a sense of betrayal in the way they consulted the doctors without warning, reflecting how they felt their expectations for retirement had been betrayed as well as how they perhaps each felt betrayed during their marriage. The hostility expressed in the negative transference enabled this couple to avoid the excruciating pain of their predicament: how to maintain their adult and sexual relationship when because of a debilitating illness, their relationship had been reduced to one like that of a parent and helpless infant. It may be that some of my difficulty in working with this couple and perhaps Kay's (the nurse auxiliary who left the sessions) reflected a wish to avoid fully confronting their pain. Perhaps too Kay's absence and my consequent loss of a therapeutic partner also enacted an aspect of how they each felt let down by the other.

## Longer therapy with an older couple

### Mr and Mrs Day – a couple who kept killing off hope

*Finding a curiosity about the unconscious*

*Despite Mr Day's passivity he co-operated providing an informative account of his history and brought some unconscious material in a dream. His response to the interpretation of the dream augured well for the therapy.*

Mr Day, a man in his early seventies was referred by his GP who was worried Mr Day was suffering from depression. A once active man, he had become more and more passive, spending most of the day sitting in an armchair at home. At first I saw Mr Day for three one-hour meetings at fortnightly intervals. He reminded me of an archetypal major general, an upright solid man, with a reddish complexion and a silver grey moustache. When I asked him about himself he straightaway talked about some of his experiences in World War Two. It seemed he had something of a breakdown whilst fighting in the trenches. He experienced a mental blackout when asked to perform a routine duty. He could not explain what had happened to him. He was promptly sent off to see a doctor in a nearby village. As he arrived at the village he noticed the local padre's house. He thought he could either go to the doctor or the padre. Instead he decided to simply go back to his platoon where no further enquiries were made about what had happened to him. He continued his career in the army without a recurrence of this troubling episode.

Mr Day was quite a raconteur and seemed to enjoy entertaining me with stories of his war exploits, including an especially frightening period when he had to clear land mines. Just prior to his blackout he had received news his fiancée had broken off their engagement. He felt devastated, but soon after started regular correspondence with a boyhood friend's sister with whom he had kept in touch. At the conclusion of the war when he came home he proposed and they soon married, despite some opposition from her family who feared he might be marrying on the rebound.

Mr Day told me about his early life. His parents had both worked 'in service' as servants in a large house. Then his father, whom he described as gentle, had made a career as a stationmaster. His mother was in poor health during his childhood and died some years before his father. He had a memory of being told his father dreamed he was hitting a rat, only to wake up and find that he was hitting his wife who was in bed beside him. Mr Day was fond of both his parents. He was very close to his sister who was his only sibling. She was a few years his senior and had died several years earlier of Parkinson's Disease. He said he had a happy childhood and marriage.

After the war he pursued training and qualified in a profession. He said he always tended to see the more negative side of things, feeling he was a pessimist. In the last few years he became lazy, was 'opting out', feeling he didn't want to do anything and didn't know why. He did little around the house and had lost interest in activities which previously he enjoyed. For example he had a talent for drawing and liked doing watercolours and making Christmas cards for his friends, but he stopped all the art work. He said his wife wore the pants, she was full of energy and she was in the driving seat, quite literally because she drove him to these appointments. Five or six years ago during a holiday, his wife said she was disappointed in him and no longer loved him. At about that time they ceased having a sexual relationship. He said he realised he'd always had to take the initiative and that she didn't really enjoy sex. In mid-life he had seen a psychiatrist who prescribed tranquilisers which Mr Day gradually 'weaned' himself off.

In the third meeting, Mr Day brought a dream in which he was travelling on the underground. He did not know in which direction to go, nor had anyone to talk to about it. His association to the dream was the story about the choice between the padre and the doctor after his blackout, when he had chosen neither. I said I thought the dream was about the choice now before him, whether to pursue some therapy with me. He was anxious that again he would choose not to do so and have no one to talk to, when perhaps it now felt more urgent to sort things out at the end of his life before he died. Mr Day said he wasn't conscious of this, but he looked interested in the interpretation. At the conclusion of this meeting I said I felt it would be better for me to see Mr Day and his wife together and, provided she agreed, for us to meet once a fortnight for an hour, on an open-ended basis. Mr Day was pleased to include his wife. He agreed to bring her to the next meeting.

## Commentary

Mr Day presents an example of someone willingly identifying himself as the problem partner, in contrast to Mrs Henderson 'for whom retirement became a nightmare' described at the beginning of the chapter, who only saw the problems in her husband. It was because of a polarised view of himself and his wife that I suspected Mr Day might be incapacitated by a projective process in the couple relationship. So I decided to extend the assessment over three sessions to explore further whether to include his wife in the sessions. I came to the view that there was a splitting process in this couple relationship in which all the interest and liveliness resided in Mrs Day, whilst Mr Day had become inert and depressed. I hypothesised that Mr Day may have been carrying some of his wife's depression, just as she was now a receptacle for his capacities. In order to address this split I thought it would be more expedient to work with them both.

Supervision helped me to see the anger expressed in Mr Day's passivity, anger perhaps with a wife who was felt to be second best, and whom he hurt by giving her the pants to wear. Though he looked the part of a major general, he may have felt ill-prepared by his gentle father for asserting himself and being openly aggressive.

An encouraging sign for psychodynamic work was Mr Day bringing a dream to the third meeting, which felt like a gift of some unconscious material. Despite his passivity, this was an important indication of an interest in and co-operation for gaining access to the unconscious. The dream indicated his need to talk but also his ambivalence about exploring the 'underground' of his mental and emotional life. In the context of being an older client the reference in Mr Day's associations to the padre, made me think of his conscious and unconscious awareness of death and therefore a greater sense of urgency to get on with talking now. His response to my interpretation of the dream was further confirmation of his readiness for therapy: he made a distinction between what was conscious and unconscious and he seemed interested in learning more about the unconscious.

## Hope and disappointment

*During these early sessions at first I felt hopeful about this couple, only to then be disappointed when they kept reporting that the therapy made no differ-*

*ence. Like Penelope of the Greek legends, they seemed to unpick the work between the sessions, but I found it difficult to confront them about this undermining process.*

Following the assessment sessions and a Christmas break Mrs Day joined her husband for the fortnightly sessions. She impressed me as a forceful woman. She wore no make-up, had grey hair which was simply cut and swept back, and she wore somewhat plain clothes. She nonetheless exuded an unmistakable sensuality, which puzzled me in the light of her husband's complaints about her disinterest in sex. She soon launched into a tirade of complaints about Mr Day whom she described as a 'vegetable', wanting her to do practically everything. Things had been 'alright' with her husband until about five years ago, though he had been very dependent on her for a long time. Her life revolved around the two dogs, one their own and an older dog which belonged to her 90 year-old mother, who had been living with them for several years. Mrs Day took the dogs for long walks each day. She felt very resentful that her husband had gradually stopped accompanying her. He looked on rather meekly during this angry speech and merely said the walks were now too much for him. Her riposte was that the less he exercised the more disabled he would become. She was obviously irritated by his concerns about his physical state and impatient that he would not extend himself, even if it did mean some discomfort. With some sadness she said she felt lonely and missed his company on the walks. She said he spent most of the time slumped in a chair. They hardly talked to one another anymore. She felt their marriage was no longer a partnership. Mr Day then spoke about the time she said she didn't love him anymore, and his hurt about that. Towards the end of this meeting Mrs Day said she felt hopeless. She asked me 'Where does this all lead?' I felt somewhat thrown because I was impressed with how open they had both been. It seemed to me they had started talking.

Over the next sessions a pattern emerged in which Mrs Day would arrive looking pained and produce numerous complaints about her husband since the previous meeting. Mr Day usually had little to say in his defence, but would look embarrassed and hurt. I often felt drawn into siding with Mrs Day against her husband, trying to urge him into life. At the same time I tried to resist this because I could see it made him withdraw into passivity.

I learned that Mrs Day's mother was French and her father was about 30 years older than her mother. Her mother sounded a forbidding figure. Mrs Day recalled an incident from her childhood in which her mother slammed the lid of the piano on her fingers. She said her mother insisted the children always went early to bed before her father came home; so fond as she was of him, she saw little of him. Mrs Day did not feel close to her mother whom she described as a cold woman. As an adult Mrs Day had been hurt by her mother's criticism. Since Mrs Day's mother came to live with them Mr and Mrs Day organised their life around her, for example rarely going out at lunch time because the mother liked to have a cooked lunch prepared for her. They had taken mother to live with them in their small bungalow when she had no longer been able to look after herself. There was now little room for either of them to pursue former hobbies and interests at home.

Mrs Day's mother tended to sit most of the day like Mr Day. She rarely spoke except to give monosyllabic replies to questions. Mrs Day excused her mother's silence as due to having spent the latter part of her life on her own. Curiously, Mrs Day, like her husband, described a childhood memory which included a rat. She talked about a time when as a young girl she looked into a small outhouse for a door key and screamed because she saw the red eyes of a rat staring at her.

For some years after they were married, Mr and Mrs Day tried to conceive without success, so they adopted a baby boy. Two years after the adoption Mrs Day gave birth to a son. During their adolescence both sons were somewhat estranged from their parents who experienced a lot of guilt about them. They felt closer to their natural son who was married with children, whereas they described their adopted son as cold and aloof. He was divorced after an unhappy marriage.

Mrs Day knew about her husband's failed engagement. She was I think rather irritated that Mr Day, throughout their marriage, kept in touch with his former fiancée. Mr Day spoke of feeling inferior to his wife, who came from a well-to-do family unlike his own. He spoke of her lack of interest in sex. She said angrily that he had left her alone for so long she was not prepared to have a physical relationship with him now.

## Commentary

The start of the work with Mr and Mrs Day shows the problems when there is a strong positive counter-transference. I was disappointed each time this couple came back complaining after I felt we had done some good work in the previous sessions. But I was unable to think about the attacks in these complaints on me and the therapy. I found it difficult to think of them attacking me, perhaps reflecting a rather idealised transference of mine onto them as older parents whom I could enjoy and who would enjoy being with me.

Supervision enabled me to eventually take up the attacks. I became more aware too of how I sometimes joined with Mrs Day in criticising her husband, just as they sometimes ganged up with each other against me. I saw the effects on this older couple of having an even older parent living with them: they were reduced to a childlike state, living as brother and sister in the presence of a tyrannical mother; and in his passivity Mr Day seemed to be in competition with his mother-in-law for his wife's attentions. In the transference I was probably experienced like this mother, impassive, tyrannical and critical of them both.

### Attacks and resentments

*After this first holiday in the therapy, the negative transference was expressed in a concerted attack on me when I seemed to represent a potent sexual couple. At the same time they continued to provoke each other, in Mrs Day's relentless criticisms of her husband and in his retaliatory passivity, with the result that they could not engage with each other in a satisfying or creative way.*

When they resumed the sessions Mr Day began by saying they weren't getting anywhere. He said the sessions were simply opening up old wounds which were hurtful, they were not uplifting nor was he feeling any better. Mrs Day said little though she looked frustrated, and appeared to agree the sessions were useless. She complained again about feeling a prisoner and having to look after her husband and her mother. Mr Day then described a time when he felt very angry with his wife. He was doing some decorating, painting a ceiling in extremely hot weather. After he had finished his wife came in and instead of any praise for his efforts she pointed out some paint which had dropped on the carpet. He was furious and had not done any painting since. At the conclusion of this session, as they were about to leave, Mr Day turned to his wife and asked her if it was convenient for them to come to the session next fortnight. I felt really put in my place!

When they returned the next fortnight, Mrs Day began by talking about a television programme they'd started watching which had some explicit sex in it. They turned it off in disgust. I made a link with how they had turned away from their own sexual relationship. Mrs Day seemed genuinely puzzled about what had gone wrong between them because they had had such an enjoyable sexual relationship, almost 'too good'. I wondered aloud whether it felt 'too good to last': if their relationship was too good then the anticipation of the end of their lives together would be too painful, so it might be preferable to end on a sour note. Later, there was some talk about the shadow of Mr Day's fiancée, like a paint stain on their relationship.

The following fortnight there was a long discussion about how they apportioned the different domestic jobs since Mr Day retired. Mrs Day seemed annoyed that Mr Day wanted to do the washing up, vacuuming and make the beds, jobs she felt were for women. Mr Day felt it was the least he could do. He rather liked doing those jobs. I felt some sympathy for Mrs Day's view that her husband wanted to take over the woman's jobs and would not do the manly work around the house. Later in supervision I could see that there was also a dispute about the nice jobs and who would do them. Mrs Day seemed to want to keep all the nice jobs to herself.

They came to the next session looking a good deal happier, and even shared a joke together. They laughed about a repair man who was working in the house during their lunch hour. He misunderstood Mr Day's question to him about whether he had had lunch, as an invitation to lunch with them. They were relieved he did not accept. Then they talked about having to keep the two dogs apart when the male dog got 'randy'. When I picked up the sexual theme, Mrs Day railed against her mother for making hurtful accusations about her being promiscuous when she was an adolescent and generally for being a critical presence in their household. Mr Day spoke of going to art lessons after he retired, and then dropping out when the teacher was critical of him. They both recalled enjoying going bowling together and then stopping for no obvious reason.

At the next session Mr Day talked at length about his career, relishing the memories in stories of his work. He said there were various changes now with the introduction of computers and other new techniques. Sadly he admitted he wouldn't be able to do the work anymore even if he were allowed back. Then they both began to argue about his reluctance to do anything now. He said activities like gardening caused him too much physical discomfort. His wife objected that by doing less and less he would become even more unfit. I found myself feeling irritated with him. I asked him why it was so important not to feel any discomfort. Mrs Day said she was particularly unhappy that he no longer joined her on the walks with the dogs. She said she couldn't share the pleasures of the walks with him. He was cross and said she didn't talk to him when she was at home. I said I felt this argument about the walks illustrated the resentment which was being passed back and forth between them.

## Commentary

In retrospect I can see a strong negative transference to me following the Easter holiday. The complaints about lack of any progress were especially virulent and for both of them I had become a critical presence drawing attention to the stains in their relationship, like the paint dropped on the carpet. Unconsciously, I think they were both laughing at me, like the repair man, for my thinking that they wanted my company. They joined together in making attacks on me who, in the transference represented a potent sexual couple, treating me as a 'randy dog' who had to be separated from its mate. With my relative youth, my holiday and having a job to return to after it, it was as though I was flaunting my potency in front of them. It would have been helpful if I could have interpreted these unconscious negative feelings towards me and shown the couple how these critical feelings were preferable to sad feelings about loss, evoked by my absence during the holiday. When Mr Day did bring some of his sad feelings about the loss of his work, they quickly became embroiled in bickering. I tended to be drawn into the argument, joining in an avoidance of the sadness about the losses in their lives so far, and about the losses which lay ahead.

The material in these sessions reveals the effects of this couple's own early experience of their parents' marriages on their relationship. They shared an intolerance of any failings in the relationship, like the paint stain on the carpet. Mrs Day couldn't seem to bear the stain without criticising Mr Day and he couldn't bear her criticism. The couple relationship was meant to make up for poor experiences of their parents' relationships. At the same time they did not know what to do with a potent couple either represented by the dogs or myself, or themselves when they were first married trying to conceive, because neither of them had much of an experience of a happy parental couple. Alternatively, the parental couples that were internalised may have been subject to internal attack because of the emotions they stirred, just as I sometimes was attacked in the transference relationship. Such attacks may have led to 'remnant' parental couples (O'Shaughnessy quoted by Fisher, 1995) in their internal worlds, which are damaged and damaging sources of identification.

## A breakthrough in the therapy

*The preceding work on Mr and Mrs Day's resentment subsequently enabled the expression of some positive feelings for each other and in the transference to me. In contrast to the previous holiday, the anticipation of loss revived by the approach of this next holiday brings some sadness.*

The next session, which I shall report in more detail, took place a month before the summer holiday. Mr and Mrs Day came back in a happier mood. They reported Mr Day had been walking a bit with Mrs Day. They had enjoyed some outings together at their church and with their son, his wife and their grandchildren. When I asked which son they were talking about, Mrs Day said their natural son. She added that their adopted son who was divorced had no children. Rather wistfully she wondered that if he had some children, then the children might have kept him and his wife together. She also said how it was better to have someone to look after, like her mother, because it helped her put up with her husband. I said I wondered if she didn't have her mother to look after, would she put up with her husband? She laughed and said that thought had occurred to her. I said perhaps Mr Day was exploiting this situation because he knew his wife wouldn't leave so long as she had to look after her mother. Mr Day replied rather sourly: 'Not consciously'.

Then Mr Day described two dreams he had since the previous meeting. In the first dream he was in a large void, a space like an aircraft hangar, with a lot of men who all looked alike. They were having stew, but there was no cutlery to eat it with. The second dream was about a 'well-constructed' Victorian house which had a basement flat going underground. Mr Day was checking the flat, the plumbing, etc., with a team of men. The dream then changed to a picture of a large building with many small cubicles which he felt were for children, and he felt very upset. He woke up and asked his wife what time it was, something he rarely did.

The hangar reminded him of one used by the navy. All the men looked like Mr Thorpe a man he had met when walking with his wife. Mr Thorpe's wife was presently in hospital with knee trouble. Mr and Mrs Day had wondered how Mr Thorpe would manage without her. Mr Day said he liked walking with Mr and Mrs Thorpe because they walked slowly and he could keep up with them, whereas Mrs Day strides ahead. Mrs Day then complained about having to look after her mother as no one else was able to do so. She was angry that she had recently strained herself doing the gardening which she had to do all by herself because her husband would not help her. It was not a partnership anymore.

I asked about the second dream. Mr Day had no associations to it, but Mrs Day said there had been accounts in the papers recently of children being locked up in a room by their parents and shut away from their friends – awful stories. Mr Day objected that he wasn't aware of having read anything like that.

I said the first dream reminded me that Mrs Day recently had to go into hospital (for a minor operation). Mr Day quickly added that he too had been into hospital for a prostrate operation which was successful, and now his medication has been reduced. I said I thought the dream was about Mr Day's thoughts about death, about who will die first and a worry that like Mr Thorpe he would be left alone. Mrs Day quickly agreed saying that she noticed in the dream there was no one to serve him the food and nothing to eat it with. She then talked about her husband's breakdown some years before when he used to follow her everywhere, even waiting outside the toilet until she came out. He used to get very worried whenever she left him. Mr Day said he still tended to feel this way. He recalled waiting with his mother-in-law for his wife to return, and getting rather upset because she was late. He said to his mother-in-law 'Come on let's put the kettle on', as though that would magically make his wife arrive. On another occasion when he was out walking with his wife and the light was beginning to fade, he temporarily lost sight of her. Then he feared something had happened to her. He felt angry when she finally came back.

I linked the second dream with the earlier interpretation, seeing it as an elaboration of the anxieties in the first one. I said that it showed the childlike feelings of being helpless and alone, stirred in the fading light at the end of his life. Another aspect that occurred to me was that so long as Mr Day could remain in a helpless and dependent state on his wife, he could feel that she would never die and leave him. But if he began to be more active then his fear was he might lose her. Reciprocally Mrs Day could feel that so long as she was needed by her husband and mother, she could never die. In other words they had reached an unconscious agreement by which they could defy death.

At the end of this session Mr Day asked me what should he do, and whether making these things conscious would help him change? I said I thought he wanted some reassurance from me and was turning to me in a helpless and dependent way. I said it was painful to face the uncertainty of who will die first and who will be left alone. I acknowledged that they were bringing these worries in order to understand more and with the hope that they could change. I finished the session by telling them of the dates for my holiday in a month's time.

In the following session they returned again with reports of no improvement. I felt particularly disappointed because I thought we had done some good work on the dreams, and had looked forward to seeing them again. They talked about the burden of having Mrs Day's mother living with them. I wondered if they were also burdened with a sense of guilt about waiting for her to die, and a secret wish that she would die. In the final session before the holiday Mr Day said he had 'thrown a wobbly' a few days before. Whilst out on his own he suddenly felt he was going to faint or pass out. I talked about the fear of death we had seen in the dreams. To my surprise, Mrs Day admitted sometimes she was afraid of having a stroke when she was out walking alone. Apparently her father had several strokes and she feared the same thing might happen to her. She also talked rather sadly about missing her husband on her walks, and not being able to share them with him. Mr Day said sorrowfully how close they had once been. They used to go to art exhibitions and instinctively knew which works of art the other liked.

I linked Mr Day's 'wobbly' with worries stirred by the holiday and the losses in their lives they were grieving, including the anticipation of their deaths. Mr Day, rather tersely asked me if he decided to go out again on his own, how would he know he wouldn't throw another wobbly? I said I thought if he came more alive in himself and to their former good relationship, then he would have to face the pain that life was coming to an end. Whereas if the relationship was awful then he would have no regrets about dying. At the end of the session he turned to me and said 'When did the rot set in?' I said the rot seemed a reference to awareness of ageing, physical decline and mortality.

## Commentary

The session reported in detail shows a breakthrough in the therapy. It was the first one, during six month's work, in which this couple acknowledged any sense of improvement. I think the turning point was when in the previous session I got hold of the resentment which they expressed to each other. Months later, in several sessions they returned to the theme of resentment and how much their consciousness of it helped them free themselves of its spoiling effects. My supervisor pointed out whenever the resentment was acknowledged. Mr Day came out of his inert state, regained his capacity to think and was able to contribute helpful thoughts in the sessions. Only later was I able to take up their resentment of me in the transference.

The dreams were gifts of unconscious material and reflected their alliance in the therapeutic work. In arriving at an interpretation of the dreams the preamble about their adoptive son's marriage which might have been saved by children, and about Mrs Day's looking after her mother, keeping her with her husband, seemed relevant associative material. It was useful too to have Mrs Day's associations because it made the dreams more clearly a shared piece of material which I was gradually able to interpret in terms of their relationship. I think my gaucherie in making a shift from interpreting the dream from Mr Day's perspective to thinking about what it revealed about the relationship, reflects a difficulty in moving from working individually, where I would focus on the transference meaning of the dream and be primarily concerned about the individual's internal world, to working with a couple, where as Warren Colman writes the focus is 'on the interaction between the couple *as an end in itself*' (Colman, 1993, p. 73). I take this focus to include the couples' shared transferences about the couple relationship and also, where it seems relevant, their individual transferences to one another and to the therapist(s).

The interpretative hypothesis about an unconscious agreement to defy death, revealed in the dreams, may also explain some of Mr and Mrs Day's resistance to the therapy in their unpicking of the work between the sessions. Evelyn Cleavely writes that 'change may be resisted because it could seem to threaten life itself, so the couple may unconsciously agree to keep hope alive but forever around the corner' (1993, p. 67).

The success of the interpretation about the dreams can be seen in the emergence of new material when Mr and Mrs Day talked of fears of each other dying as well as their own fears of death, something I was astonished to hear from Mrs Day who seemed to take pride in her youthfulness and vigour. Some of the anxieties, especially the infantile fears of being abandoned, were doubtless provoked by the approach of my summer holiday. But I think the infantile fears of dependency were intensified by this older couple's awareness of the 'rot' of physical decline. I felt they approached these worries with more tolerance for sad feelings as a result of the work we had been able to do.

They returned from the summer holiday with the same complaints as previously. I had some more time available and decided to offer them weekly sessions because I felt the gap between the fortnightly sessions was too long. We still struggled with a great deal of negativity which was largely expressed in their grievances that nothing was changing between them. I was struck by the references they both made to rats in the accounts of their early lives, which I think resonated with something quite cruel going on between them, and between them and me. I was eventually able to take up their spoiling attacks in a session before Christmas when they protested about some young kids who had been killing birds with peashooters. I talked about the kids in the room who were shooting at me and our work, killing off any hope. Mr Day said he felt things went bad between them 20 years earlier when their boys left home, and they were thrown back on themselves. The complaints lessened. Evidence of further change came after Christmas when they returned with a plan for a holiday. Mrs Day had found a local authority home where her mother could stay which would enable them to go away on their own, something they had not done for a very long time.

## Summary

Adversity in later life, which may have been borne more easily at earlier times, places strains and demands on older couples' relationships because it can galvanise around the losses and other difficulties experienced in ageing. Retirement and children leaving home mean that the older couple are thrown together, often much more intensely than ever before, perhaps having to manage illness and frailty in themselves, their partner or an older parent or parents. Old grievances may be clung to as a way of trying to ease the pain and helplessness in witnessing physical and mental decline in one's partner or oneself, and becoming a nurse or a patient, instead of a lover. Enduring psychological problems, like depression, in one partner may intensify, and the other partner may find it harder to bear in the face of his or her own vulnerabilities connected with ageing.

The couple therapist, working singly or with another therapist, needs to monitor the individual transferences between the couple and to the therapist(s), and also attend to the transference onto the therapist's relationship in order to understand unconscious aspects of the couple's relationship. When one member of a couple is identified as the problem in the relationship, projective identification may mean that the partner is carrying feelings that the other finds unmanageable; and projective identification may be being used intrusively to possess and control because of underlying fears of dependency and loss. With ageing, the revival of feelings of helplessness and dependency may also bring echoes of early unresolved Oedipal issues and difficulties around inclusion and exclusion, which may hook into a couple's history of jealousies and betrayals, and which may be played out in the relationships with the therapist(s). Returning to old quarrels, hurts and resentments may be preferable to sadness and sorrow about loss and incapacity, and facing the final loss and abandonment brought by the death of one's partner.

# 6

# GROUPS FOR VERY FRAIL OLDER
# PEOPLE AND THEIR CARERS

## Introduction

Group therapy for older people is well-established, and Sandra Evans (2004b) a group-analyst and old age psychiatrist, has provided a comprehensive review of its history and development. Caroline Garland (2007) who has written in detail about a psychoanalytic approach to groups and group therapy 'in the third age', describes the value of mixed age groups and gives a vivid example of an older woman benefiting from being in a therapy group with much younger people. Garland recognises that in settings such as residential care, mixed age groups are not usually possible, but she emphasises the importance of doing something and of not colluding with passivity in older people which she calls ' the curse of old age'. She observes that through passivity 'the silent resentment of old age itself can communicate itself both consciously and unconsciously to everyone within range, leading to an equally silent resentment at having to shoulder the burden of caring' (p. 106).

This chapter describes an attempt to address such passivity by establishing groups for very frail older people and their carers in long stay care. The majority of older people in long stay or 'continuing' care tend to be in their seventies or eighties and have multiple illnesses which leave them severely disabled and highly dependent. The groups were established for older people on continuing care wards which were part of an NHS hospital. These continuing care patients and nursing staff were later transferred to small residential nursing homes managed by the private sector (Terry, 1998). Most of these patients were wheelchair bound; just a very few could walk but only with the help of the staff. Nearly half had suffered from strokes and a third from dementia. A smaller proportion had rheumatoid arthritis, epilepsy, fractures or diabetes. Some had speech impairments or were unable to speak or eat or swallow. Many were incontinent. Nearly a fifth had hearing and visual problems. Few were terminally ill, but all would remain in care until they died. Several had been on the wards for over ten years.

An observational study of older people in continuing care settings of hospitals and nursing homes (Clark and Bowling, 1989) has confirmed previous research in this area, and both my clinical experience of these settings and the comments about passivity quoted above. The study found a lack of contact between older patients, only occasional 'comments' passed between staff and patients and rather a lot of negative 'bickering' interactions on wards. A high proportion of these older people were described as detached, 'showing no bias or emotional involvement, disinterested, disconnected'. The study concluded that despite the various 'flexible' philosophies of hospitals or homes, 'caring practices are characterised by routinisation and control'. I witnessed how staff 'serviced' the patients in rigid regimes of getting them out of bed in the mornings, feeding, 'toileting' and taking them to the day-room or the activity ward and back to bed in the early evening.

The groups I shall describe involved weekly one-hour meetings with all the older people and staff on a continuing care ward. In establishing the groups my hope was to alleviate some of the factors which contribute to the deadly institutionalisation. When I decided to establish the group meetings I gained some discomfiting personal insight into some of the obstacles against contact and interaction on these wards. I realised that I much preferred to simply meet the care staff in 'support' groups in meetings such as I describe in Chapter 9, rather than have direct contact with the older people for whom they cared. Then, having overcome my conspicuous procrastination in starting the group meetings for older patients and staff, I found myself colluding, for a while, with a selection process for the groups in which the more disabled and 'difficult' patients were excluded.

I met with the patients individually to explain the *purpose of the groups*: an opportunity to discuss some of their life experiences, aspects of living on the ward, thoughts and feelings about approaching the end of their lives, even their dreams. I assured them they did not have to attend; but if they later changed their minds and wanted to attend they would be welcome, or if they agreed to attend they could later choose to discontinue. Some of the patients hardly seemed to take in what I said about the groups, but no one objected. A few were keen, saying it was a good idea and giving me the impression that they felt they would be able to help other patients by stories of their interesting lives.

When I spoke individually to the previously unselected patients, it was painfully clear why many of these patients had not been suggested earlier. They tended to be much more withdrawn, some were deaf, some had lost their speech and others were incoherent and confused. I found several of them physically smelly and repulsive; some were unable to sit in wheelchairs and instead were half sitting, half lying in 'bean bag' cradle chairs.

I saw that my reluctance to become emotionally engaged with the long stay patients was an important and probably unconscious aspect of how most of the staff felt. Despite my determination to overcome such feelings, my continued procrastination brought home to me the strength of the underlying dread that the anticipation of the contact provoked. This process helped me understand why staff would so often say they didn't have time to spend talking to the patients. Of course there were real difficulties because of the heavy work load and staff shortages, but I think there were worries about spending time with the patients – worries with which I also struggled.

Much of the staff's work was devoted to the physical care and well-being of these 'heavily dependent' patients. There were a few staff responsible for 'activities' which took place in a special unit away from the wards where patients could go during the day if they wished. This arrangement perpetuated a split between what Miller and Gwynne (1973) have identified as a 'warehousing' ideology, on the wards, which aims to prolong life, and a 'horticultural' ideology which aims to promote independence in activities which usually happen elsewhere. I think the staff were apprehensive about being more in touch with their patients' feelings about living such reduced lives. Further, if they became more involved trying to help their patients utilise to the full their remaining capacities then they would be confronted with the dreadful limits of what was possible for these older people.

All the wards were named after fortified castles. I shall describe group meetings from a ward I shall call 'Warwick' ward. There were usually 20 patients on the ward, and Warwick was typical in that about two-thirds were women. For the first five weeks there were 8–10 'selected' patients in the group and when the unselected patients joined the group usually 15–18 patients attended the meetings each week. The meetings were held in the day-room. Three patients stopped attending the meetings, two quite openly, the other in collusion with her relatives who timed their weekly visit to coincide with the meetings. Sometimes patients remained on the ward because they were too ill. About four of the five or six staff on duty attended, not always willingly, but sometimes under pressure from the ward sister and the hospital manager who were keen to support the meetings. Some staff stayed on the ward to look after those who did not attend.

About half the patients were seated in their wheelchairs, others were in hospital armchairs and just one or two in easy chairs brought from their own homes. They were arranged in a rectangular configuration in one half of the day-room because two obscuring columns prevented us sitting in a circle. The staff would often have some patients seated in front of the columns when I arrived. I think they regarded my insistence on patients being seated so as to be able to see one another, as a funny eccentricity. When the staff rearranged the patients so they could see, the patients showed little reaction, as if it did not matter one way or the other. Only two of the patients had electric wheelchairs and could position themselves.

It took some time for the staff to stop questioning and cajoling the patients to speak, especially at the beginning of meetings or when there were silences. In most meetings few of the patients spoke but I tried to encourage an attitude of waiting for patients to speak, and for staff to speak about their own thoughts and feelings. However, often when I arrived, one of the patients, Mrs Bradford, a woman with thick swollen legs, would say in a voice like a school mistress' and full of mockery: 'Be quiet, Mr Terry has come to speak to us!'

## The group meetings

### Reaching anger beneath passivity

*An interpretation of the patients' anger enabled them to give voice to some of their complaints and grief. In subsequent meetings there was some liveliness and then closeness through the sharing of sad feelings.*

I began by reminding the group of the purpose of the meeting. Two of the patients, Mr Potter and Mrs Brown, talked briefly about their lives in a rather contented way. Both concluded by expressing their gratitude to the staff for looking after them. The staff started urging other patients to speak which made me feel angry. I said it was probably difficult for the patients to talk about their feelings if they felt they had to be good and grateful to the staff, especially if they were feeling angry and helpless about having to end their lives living in this way.

One of the men, Mr Wood seemed to agree with me. He was a large man, dwarfing his wheelchair in which he sat slumped to one side. His spectacles were a bit lopsided and he peered through them with difficulty. There were traces of spilled food on his clothing. He gave me the impression of following everything very closely. Most of his speech was incomprehensible to me because it was slurred. The ward sister, Shirley, who could understand him, repeated what he said. He spoke at length about his admission to the hospital and his anger about not being told he was to be admitted for a long stay. He thought he was coming to the ward for a short stay.

In the second meeting Mr Potter, who had severe arthritis and Parkinson's Disease, talked in more detail about his life and his frustration now at being so helpless. He tried to make some links between himself and others in the group. He mentioned having been a market gardener and knowing Mrs Cooper who was seated opposite him. A slight woman with curly grey hair, she appeared asleep with her eyes closed and her head buried in her chest. She did not respond to Mr Potter. She remained silent and as if asleep for most of the time in the first five meetings. (Mrs Cooper finally spoke in the sixth meeting when the unselected patients joined the group. She talked about how much she missed another woman patient who had died at least a year before.)

At the third meeting I noticed that all the women had been seated together and were facing the men. One of the more active women, Mrs Butler, who had an electric wheelchair, seemed to be flirting with Mr Roberts who was severely disabled. He seemed to have no speech and was propped up by several pillows in his chair. Mrs Butler kept gesturing towards him and giggling with some of the other women. He responded with a toothless grin. There was little talk except from staff who were quizzing the patients to try to get them to speak. Several patients appeared asleep and some others stared into space. I was reminded of a dance with young women and men lined up opposite each other giggling in embarrassment. I spoke about how painful it must be for the patients to be there like this, as if at a dance but no longer able to dance.

After a while, Mr Holdsworth, who had not previously spoken in the meetings, talked about having been a piano player. He was a small thin man with sunken cheeks and a soft breathless voice. He was supported by pillows and usually appeared asleep, confused or withdrawn. In my preliminary discussions with the staff they had shown me some early photos of him at the piano with his band and on his wedding day, then a dapper bright-eyed fellow. He spoke briefly with great effort. He held up his hands revealing long elegant fingers. Mrs Ferguson, a woman with hearing difficulties, often struggling in vain with her hearing aid, looked intently at Mr Holdsworth's hands. She said they were the hands of a pianist. He replied he could no longer play the piano, and sobbed bitterly.

## Commentary

I think these early meetings show how difficult it is for older patients to express their negative feelings, especially their anger when they are so frail and dependent on their carers. My interpretation of the anger, which I understood from my counter-transference, seemed to free some of the patients of the pressure to be on their best behaviour, pleased and contented. It was also apparent how reluctant some of the patients were about making contact with one another. Mrs Cooper's expression of grief about missing another patient, illustrates how the patients sometimes withdrew from contact rather than face the pain of more losses. When there was some lively contact between the patients as in the 'dance' at the third meeting, the contact brought painful reminders of past lives and poignant feelings of sadness – a telling illustration of the pain that is avoided by the passivity and withdrawal. Afterwards there were complaints from the staff that this meeting was upsetting. The complaints expressed their discomfort about the sadness which followed some contact between the patients and illustrates why, unwittingly, in order to avoid sad feelings staff may collude in the passivity on the ward.

### The torment of illness and relentless loss

*When the non-selected, more severely disabled patients were included in the meetings, there was an introduction of cruelty and torment which intensified as the first holiday neared. Following interpretations about feelings of loss stirred by the holiday, some tranquillity returned and the patients were able to talk about how much they missed the staff when the staff were absent.*

From the fifth meeting all the patients on the ward were included in the meetings. At this and the next, sixth meeting, a cruel scenario was enacted involving Mrs Bradford, a new, relatively younger and fitter patient and Miss Smith, one of the oldest, a woman in her nineties. Both had not previously been in the meetings. Mrs Bradford was the patient with swollen legs who spoke like a school mistress and told patients to be quiet when I arrived. Miss Smith, a small wrinkled lady, like a wizened version of Punch and Judy, sat regally with legs outstretched on a stool. Sometimes she called for her lost cat which was given away when she came into hospital and sometimes she asked for 'Emily', who was assumed to be her sister. Just as she apparently did on the ward, she talked at length to no one, though seeming to make eye contact with her neighbours, often smiling and gracious. Much of her talk made no sense because it seemed to be fragments of past conversations. Other patients and staff were spoken to as if they were people from her past. She didn't wait for replies, or if replies were given then they were ignored or fitted into her reconstructed conversations.

Mrs Bradford joined in Miss Smith's conversations so as to make fun of her and amuse the others, especially the staff who laughed with her. At times she would get angry with Miss Smith's incessant talk and tell her to shut up. Or, as a theatrical aside, she would exclaim how sad it was to see this 'old dear' talking in this way. I thought it a cruel parody of how the patients felt humoured by the staff. I talked about how horrible it must be to feel ridiculed for being old and helpless, as though the patients had always been old and the staff would always be young.

In the seventh meeting, as we approached a first break in the meetings for the summer holiday, the ward sister who had attended regularly, was absent. The meeting was dominated by Miss Smith and Mrs Frost who sat alongside her. Miss Smith was again replaying old conversations. From time to time, Mrs Frost who had not spoken before and who sat with eyes closed as if asleep, would suddenly lurch forward, as though woken from the dead, eyes wide open and shrieking apparently in response to Miss Smith. Her words were incomprehensible because of a mixture of slurred and confused speech. Only in its intonation did it sound like a reply to Miss Smith who seemed to be enjoying taunting Mrs Frost. This mad duet went on for some time. I felt helpless, tormented and that listening to this would drive me crazy. Eventually I was able to say how tormented the patients must feel to be so abandoned by their families, friends and staff such as myself who go on holiday.

Just before the eighth meeting Mr Holdsworth, the pianist, died. After some time had elapsed in the meeting without any mention of his death, I spoke of it and the feelings it might have stirred. There was little reaction from the patients. Instead Miss Smith held forth again, immersing us in her imaginary conversations. I interpreted this as a retreat from the awful feelings of abandonment associated with the coming holiday. One of the senior nurses, Ella, angrily disagreed. She told me my holiday was not so important to the patients. After all she was Miss Smith's keyworker, and Miss Smith did not miss *her* when she went on holiday because she knew there would be someone else to look after her!

Later, Ella said she did not agree with my remarks about Mr Holdsworth's death. She herself felt it was not so much his death which upset the patients and staff because most of the patients and staff were not involved with him, but it was more that his death reminded her and others of folks they had lost. I agreed and thanked her.

When the meetings resumed after a five-week summer break, there was a new patient on the ward, Mrs Shorter, who had become blind late in life. She sat in an armchair, quite immobile, her head tilted back staring at the ceiling but constantly calling out 'Nurse, nurse, will you help me?' It did not seem to matter who replied, staff or patients, she did not know what she wanted and would soon call out again in the same plaintive way. She was befriended by Mrs James, a tiny woman, hard of hearing and with strong spectacles which magnified her eyes. Mrs James had not spoken previously. She was sitting next to Mrs Shorter, whom she kept reassuring, saying, in slightly slurred speech, that she would help her.

Later, Mrs James started staring at Mrs Bradford, who became angry, objecting to being stared at, even though Mrs James explained that she recognised her because she had a relative who had been a postman and knew Mrs Bradford. This was only the second time there had been any explicit connection made between these patients from links with their lives before they came into hospital, despite all coming from the local area. Mrs Bradford and Mrs James had been on the ward together for at least two months before this acknowledgement and then it was unwelcome.

At the next meeting two of the patients, Mrs Bradford and Mrs Frost, were unexpectedly brought back from a week's holiday at a seaside resort. Apparently they had been too much for the holiday staff to manage. Mrs Frost shrieked throughout the meeting, as she had done before, again lurching forward from her chair, eyes wide open as if she had seen a ghost, calling out incomprehensibly. The staff mentioned that her companion, an older man who visited her regularly and who had gone with her on the holiday, had stayed on. I talked about how much she must have missed him, and then she did seem to calm a little. Later, Mr Potter spoke of missing the permanent staff when they were away. He said he then had to put up with 'youngsters' who, when they handled him, didn't know him and his 'aches and pains'. Mr Wood seemed to agree, but his slurred speech was hard to understand. Sister Shirley, who sat alongside him, realised he was referring to missing her when was she absent from these meetings. She looked puzzled and I reminded her that she had been away for the last two meetings before the summer holiday. She was deeply touched.

## Commentary

When all the patients were included in the meetings it was clear that what had previously been left out was something quite torturing represented by Miss Smith's and Mrs Frost's disturbing dialogue. It is difficult, if not impossible to disentangle the organic effects of the patients' illnesses from the psychological elaborations of them, but nonetheless it is important to give some thought to the psychological components. On all the wards there were patients like Miss Smith or Mrs Frost, who appear to be in a world of their own, reliving past conversations and who can too easily be dismissed as suffering from an organic impairment like dementia. Just as Valerie Sinason (1986) has observed in some mentally handicapped patients, I think some of these older patients have developed psychotic defences against the trauma of debilitating illnesses. They suffer the trauma which Winnicott described, in relation to birth, of the 'intolerable nature of experiencing something without any knowledge of when it will end' (quoted by Sinason, 1986, p. 150). Such trauma can happen late in life because these older people have no certainty about how long it will be until their suffering is terminated by death. Perhaps longed for as a release from suffering, death may also be feared and such fears may summon psychotic defences. Pearl King found that sometimes fears of death are avoided by a retreat into psychosis because in her analysis of some older patients she discovered: 'Unconsciously they link mental health with being alive and if they can manage not to be part of life they will not die' (1980, p. 159).

I find Robert Hinshelwood's concept of 'dramatization' helpful in thinking about the apparently meaningless exchanges between Miss Smith and others in the meetings. Hinshelwood has described 'dramatizations' in group work in therapeutic communities as an 'enactment of the anxieties and defences against them' by the members of those communities (1987, p. 75). In the meetings preceding the first holiday break, I felt Miss Smith and Mrs Bradford, on behalf of all the patients, were engaged in a portrayal of the way staff can humour and infantilise these 'old dears' and how the patients can collude with the staff to maintain such defences. The staff can project their own helplessness, dependency and sense of worthlessness into their patients, who as Simon Biggs (1989) points out, are scarcely in a position to challenge such projections. In the next chapter I continue an examination of these counter-transference problems.

The infantile dependency relationship that staff experienced in their childhood can be reversed with their older patients. Unresolved conflicts with their own ageing parents, or grandparents, can be acted out by staff. The staff often use their defences to maintain a split between the old patients and the young staff which protects them from the terror of recognising that one day they too might be old and incapacitated like their patients. Such splits may fuel envy in these disabled patients when all the capacities are felt to be located in the staff who can walk away from them and return to their own homes and families. Mrs Bradford, the patient with swollen legs and feet, often unable to wear shoes let alone walk, would taunt the staff saying 'How would you like to be in my shoes?', knowing too well the awful spectre she was of what old age might hold in store for the staff.

The tormenting dialogues, which seemed to reach a mad crescendo as the holiday got nearer, passed on something of the patients' experience of hospital which they felt would drive them crazy: for example how so many comings and goings provoke unbearable feelings about past, present and future loss. Ella's reaction to my interpretation about the patients' feelings of loss stirred by Mr Holdworth's death and the coming holiday shows some of the staff's reluctance to recognise their importance to the patients, and the importance of the patients to them. Some understanding of Ella's reluctance to consider her importance to her patients emerged later. Ella told me that when she was first training she became very attached to a particular older patient. When this patient died Ella was inconsolable. I felt she was telling me she would never let this happen again because of the terrible pain of the loss. At seminars I conducted for staff I encountered strong resistance to a seminar on death and bereavement drawing on a chapter from Doris Lessing's *The Diaries of Jane Sommers* (1984). The diaries describe a young woman's relationship with an older woman who is admitted into long stay care and subsequently dies there. The seminar had to be repeatedly cancelled because of staff difficulties in attending. One carer openly admitted she wouldn't be coming because she couldn't 'handle bereavement'.

Not only is staff relentlessly faced with the deaths of their patients but these deaths bring them up against their unconscious infantile fears of parents dying and awareness of their own mortality. The denial of death never ceases to amaze me, most of all in myself. I arrived at one ward meeting aware of several empty chairs. On my way through the ward I had passed an empty bed of a woman I knew to have been dying. Few people spoke in the meeting, except for Miss Smith who dominated it with her usual meanderings into the past. Not until the meeting was over, as I walked away with one of the staff and asked about the missing patients, did I allow myself to know about the deaths. I think Mrs Bradford cruelly recognised that the patients, whose shoes the staff would certainly not like to be in, are 'bringers of ambivalent news' (Biggs, 1989, p. 47), because they bring news of ageing, physical decline, impairment and death.

Regimes of 'routinisation and control' and the traditional shift system which ensures staff are constantly changing, despite the commitment to a 'person centred' approach, are examples of 'social systems' which protect staff against feelings from closer involvement with their patients (Menzies-Lyth, 1960). In such ways they unconsciously defend themselves against the guilt at not providing the 24-hour-a-day familial care that these patients long for (Martindale, 1989b), and against the pain of attachments to patients who will die. Staff can be the recipients of projected unwanted feelings from their patients, particularly their sense of worthlessness. Those who work with older people are also affected by ageist attitudes from a society in which working with older people tends to be at the bottom of the professional ladder and old people are seen as 'non-productive or non-potentially' members of society, (Biggs, 1989).

## Closeness from a song of love and death

*My counter-transference suggested different motives for community singing in two meetings: in the first the singing contributed to the splitting between staff and patients and in the second it brought some closeness. The approach of a holiday break again stirred persecutory exchanges in the meetings.*

Two weeks later, the meeting was again dominated by the blind patient, Mrs Shorter. She called out repeatedly 'Nurse, nurse, will you help me?' Mrs Bradford kept replying in a humouring tone of voice offering her blatantly false promises. For example she offered to take Mrs Shorter to visit her sister. Mrs Shorter replied in an equally disingenuous way 'Oh will you, how nice'. It appeared to me a cruel parody of staff offering empty comfort to these patients only to ridicule and triumph over them.

Somewhat later, Mrs Shorter, who had a pleasant singing voice, was urged to sing. She obliged and others, even Miss Smith, joined in singing songs such as *'Now is the hour, when we must say good-bye'*, *'Keep the home fires burning…'* and *'I've got a lovely bunch of coconuts'*. I became increasingly uncomfortable about this singsong. It seemed an awful caricature of what old folks are supposed to do. At the same time I felt I couldn't say this because it would be spoiling the fun. After the singsong I noticed one of the men, Mr Russell, a man suffering with Parkinson's Disease, dementia and poor vision, lean over from his chair and start fondling Miss Smith's breasts, until he was stopped by one of the staff. Later, one of the patients and staff talked of arranging 'tea and crumpets', in a rather teasing way because there seemed to be no intention of having such a tea. Then sister Shirley rather flirtatiously described my appearance to Mrs Shorter. I felt we were having a 'bit of crumpet', and that the staff were like adolescents flaunting their sexuality at old, impotent parents.

Six weeks later I introduced a microphone into the meetings because I was worried about the patients with hearing problems and those whose speech was faint. I hoped a mike might help, but feared it could be inhibiting. To my relief it was greeted with much gaiety. Mrs Cooper, who rarely spoke, announced through the mike that she thought we were all 'barmy' and giggled. Mr Potter graciously asked Mrs Shorter if she would sing him a song and there followed some playful banter between them about his request. She consented and somewhat haltingly, with sister joining in to help her, sang 'Danny Boy'. A little later we noticed that Mrs Shorter was singing the song again, quietly to herself, this time word perfect and with great feeling. With the aid of the mike we were all able to hear a moving rendition. I felt a heartrending sadness. Staff and patients were in tears.

Later in this meeting I noticed Mrs Jones, a stroke patient who suffered from dementia, was masturbating. Sister was telling her to stop. When I wondered aloud about the masturbation, some of the staff looked disapprovingly at me. But then one of the younger staff described his experience of working with young male amputees in a nursing home where they brought in young women to masturbate them. Towards the end of the meeting Mrs Shorter asked if Mr Wood had lived in a certain street near her home. Mr Wood confirmed he had and Mrs Shorter, who was now blind, said she could remember seeing him. I found this a deeply moving session and later heard that staff and patients thought so too.

Lastly, I would like to describe two meetings which occurred after a mid-term break as we neared the Christmas holiday. Mrs Shorter was again the focus in both meetings, calling out in a repetitive and tormenting way 'Nurse, nurse, can you help me?' In one of these meetings she was seated alongside Miss Smith who was repeating her imaginary conversations which became enmeshed with Mrs Shorter's plaintive refrain. The result was that Mrs Shorter appeared to believe that Miss Smith's sister 'Emily' would be taking her out for a walk and she offered to introduce her own sister to 'Emily'. Miss Smith seemed to enjoy this confusion but also grew impatient with Mrs Shorter, at times telling her to 'Shut up!' much to the merriment of staff and patients.

The next meeting continued in the same vein, except that Mrs Shorter was alongside an auxiliary nurse who stuffed marshmallows or thrust a beaker of cold tea in Mrs Shorter's mouth to silence her. Whenever Mrs Shorter was asked what she wanted she kept saying she was frightened but didn't know what she was frightened about. There was increasing rage with her. Mrs Bradford joined in telling her to 'Shut up!' Other patients and staff taunted her. She seemed unaffected, as though she didn't hear or only heard what suited her. When the auxiliary teased her by offering her 'scotch (whisky) and chocolates', she declined the scotch but accepted the chocolates, apparently not bothered when they were not produced. One of the younger staff said he was surprised I did not get angry like they did when she talked this way, day in and day out. After the meeting I felt I had made some harsh interpretations. When they were ignored by patients and staff I seemed driven to try even harder.

## Commentary

I felt a considerable contrast between the moods of the singing in the two meetings. The first sing-song was preceded by a mocking conversation between Mrs Shorter and Mrs Bradford which again seemed a portrayal of the way patients felt they were humoured by staff. The sing-song seemed an enactment of a stereotype of old age. It reminded me of the way Sinason (1986, p. 132) describes a handicapped child choosing to behave like the 'village idiot' and 'make everyone laugh (rather) than to expose the unbearable discrepancy between normal and not normal'. So too these older patients can present themselves as happy clowns, or sweet old dears, who don't mind what's happened to them, happily engaging in a community sing-song.

In the meeting in which I introduced the microphone I think the patients were touched by my concern about the hearing difficulties and my attempt to do something about it. Some liveliness and humour brought reminders of previous happiness and sadness which Mrs Shorter expressed in her beautiful song – a song of love and the anticipation of death. The quality of the closeness in this meeting was demonstrable in the link made between two of the patients. Mrs Shorter remembered seeing Mr Wood in the past when she was sighted. This was the first time such an acknowledgment was welcomed.

Sexuality was a theme in both meetings. In the first I thought the staff were flaunting their sexuality in front of the patients at the same time as prohibiting Mr Russell's groping. This enabled a split between the sexually potent staff and the old impotent patients. By contrast some of the staff's comments about masturbation in the second meeting had more of a quality of concern and even identification with the patients. I had mixed views about Mrs Jones masturbating, on the one hand sex and death seem so inextricably linked as in the song and on the other it was perhaps used to lift us over the sad feelings. It was also a reminder of the horrible lack of privacy these patients endure on the wards.

The last two meetings show a very different, persecutory atmosphere. In these meetings Mrs Shorter's plaintive refrain 'Nurse, nurse, will you help me?' was tormenting and succeeded in provoking anger and ridicule. When patients like Mrs Shorter are provocative in this way, I think an aspect is to try to overcome their sense of no longer being in control of their lives and feeling so helpless and dependent. These provocations contributed to maintaining a paranoid-schizoid culture in the meeting. My inclination to make harsh interpretations shows how I was drawn into this culture. When I reflected on this in supervision I understood that the abrasive exchanges in the meetings left no room for sad and sorrowful feelings. Perhaps the depressive feelings in the beauty and sadness of Mrs Shorter's song were too difficult to sustain, especially faced with painful feelings stirred by the approach of Christmas. Although I had suggested Mrs Shorter was afraid of dying and that this must have been a fear shared by many there, the interpretation was lost in the tormenting dynamic of the meeting. When Mrs Shorter died unexpectedly a few weeks later, I reminded the meeting of her song which had so painfully anticipated her death:

Oh Danny Boy the pipes, the pipes are calling
From glen to glen and down the mountain side,
The summer's gone and all the roses falling
It's you, it's you must go and I must bide
But come ye back when summer's in the meadow
Or when the valley's hushed and white with snow
And I'll be here in sunshine or in shadow
Oh Danny Boy, oh Danny Boy I love you so.

But when ye come and all the flowers are dying
If I am dead, as dead I well may be
Ye'll come and find the place where I am lying
And kneel and say Ave there for me
And I shall hear, though soft you tread above me,
And all my grave will warmer, sweeter be
For you will bend and tell me that you love me
And I shall sleep in peace until you come to me.

Words by Fred E. Weatherby

## Patient and staff reaction to the group meetings

Every few months I met the staff separately to discuss their feelings about the meetings. For the first several months the staff complained that the meetings were 'dull', 'boring' and 'depressing'. They were clearly annoyed with me for not introducing topics for discussion or questioning the patients. They reported the patients said the groups were a 'waste of time' and it was 'scandalous' that I should be paid. Some of the senior nurses objected that I was upsetting their staff.

Six months after starting the meetings, I was surprised by a shift in the staff attitude. A senior nurse, Ella, said how she had changed her mind about the meetings. She felt the patients were talking more. She described how differently she had come to see Mr Wood, a stroke patient with slurred speech. Previously she hadn't thought much of him but now she could see that there was a lot to him. I also heard that one of the patients, Mrs Ferguson, who suffered from Parkinson's Disease, said to the ward sister: 'My eyes aren't shutting so much, do you think it could be because of the groups?' She had previously attributed her shutting eyelids to the Parkinson's Disease. I felt cheered by this report because the meetings had perhaps offered this woman another way of thinking about herself and made it more bearable to open her eyes to what was around her. However, the week after I heard this she was seated opposite me in the meeting, her eyes firmly shut! Twelve months later the staff were again quite negative, saying the meetings were just me going on about death all the time.

## Summary

Several years after establishing these groups, each time I walked down the long central corridor of the hospital to one of the patient and staff group meetings, I was aware I was still filled with dread. It didn't get any easier. Yet, when I started writing about this work, it was drawn to my attention that I rather took for granted the experience and learning which helped me establish and sustain the groups. I can see this may be a personal issue, but I think that I became identified with my older patients. Physical and mental decline in old age and current social attitudes towards older people mean experience and wisdom can be overlooked. At the same time these personal resources enable older patients to endure what would otherwise be unendurable.

The development of the groups illustrates my considerable ambivalence, particularly about becoming more involved with these very frail older people. It was thinking about my counter-transference which inspired the establishment of the patient and staff meetings, and enabled me to continue. It meant recognising that alongside my conscious interest and enthusiasm there was unconscious fear and even hatred of these older patients.

A central part of my recurring dread was connected with fears of death aroused by contact with the patients. Then in mid-life, I was struck by an image from Elliot Jaques' paper on 'Death and the mid-life crisis' where he describes a dream from one of his analytical patients which he found 'typifies unconscious fear and experience of death'. In the dream the patient was lying dead in a coffin, sliced up though connected with a thread of nerve to her brain and so able to experience everything, knowing she was dead but unable to speak or move (1965, p. 236). This image in the dream corresponds with the actual physical state of some very ill and incapacitated older people and may be represented most terrifyingly in advanced stages of dementia. Close contact with these older patients is equivalent to being confronted with the actuality of one's own worst phantasy of death. Unconscious phantasy and reality thus become indistinguishable. The trauma involved is similar to that faced by survivors of disasters who are brought face-to-face with their own and others' deaths. Psychoanalytic work with survivors has found that the long-term effects of disasters include difficulties in symbolic thinking because 'thought, imagination and phantasy can no longer be experienced confidently as distinct from external reality' and this causes problems for therapeutic work (Garland, 1991, p. 509). Thus, my own and carers' and patients' difficulties in thinking are very likely connected with phantasies of death being concretely experienced in the reality of the patients' physical and mental conditions.

Another source of attack on thinking was envy, conscious and unconscious, from patients and staff. I could come and go, unlike the patients and the staff who spent many hours on the ward. When the young auxiliary asked how I could bear Mrs Shorter's plaintive cries without getting angry, the uncomfortable knowledge in the question was that it was easier for me because I only had to put up with it for one hour a week. How can carers bear the contact for hours each day, day after day? I believe they can be helped to bear it when their feelings are being thought about and understood.

Much of the staff's concern was about the patients' physical condition. I felt my role was to introduce some thinking about the patients' and staff's feelings. What was most difficult was to hold in mind an awareness of the physical and emotional states of the patients, and not knowing how these states influence each other. I found it hard to take in the medical details of the patients' illnesses, and to stomach the sight, sound and smell of their physical states. I am full of admiration for the loving care the staff provides for their patients. What enabled me to continue challenging the defences against more involvement was the realisation that these defences rob the staff of the satisfaction of the reparative wishes that bring them and myself, to the work.

Sometimes the poor physical state of the patients and their under-standable envy contributed to a persecutory atmosphere which avoided grieving, especially about dying. I was aware of sometimes being drawn into this avoidance by making interpretations which could feel critical of staff and patients. My supervisor helped me be aware of a pressure to be active and perform in some way, instead of simply being with the patients and staff. I had to resist the wish to urge these patients back into health and life, which as Dorothy Judd (1989, p. 148) points out would be to deny what remains of their dying life and to deny their sadness. Simply being with the patients means facing a depressive view of death, confronting a loneliness 'felt to be without remedy' (Pasquali, 1993, p. 187), and recognising that whatever hopes may be attached to religious beliefs or life extending through the next generations or one's works, 'death is felt as a void' (p. 189).

It's when I sat quietly with these patients that I began to feel most like them, old and decrepit. Ruth Porter in a paper on psychoanalytic psychotherapy in a geriatric unit, draws attention to the need to distinguish the patients' feelings about the damage to their external and internal body image, consequent upon their illnesses, from the worries about physical health stirred in the counter-transference (1991, p. 484). It can be no coincidence that after starting this work, for some time I was more concerned about my health and felt more ill, though not actually ill, than in any previous work setting. On a couple of occasions, after leaving the wards to go to a meeting with colleagues in the clinical psychology department, I was embarrassed to find myself dishevelled and spilling food. In one group meeting a new patient repeatedly shouted at me: 'Get out!' I felt humiliated, hurt, terribly unwanted and that I'd better keep my head down and my mouth shut. A painful evocation of how many of these older patients can feel.

Surrounded by so much illness and damage and despair, I think the experience for patients and carers in their internal worlds is that destructive feelings have got the upper hand. The moving rendition of *Danny Boy* brought poignant beauty and sadness when it was possible to regain some confidence in loved and loving internal and external figures, appreciate their beauty and sorrowfully anticipate their loss. It makes me think of Donald Meltzer's work in *The Apprehension of*

*Beauty*, where he described the infant as being overwhelmed by the mother's beauty – particularly meaning all the love and care she provides – and by the awareness of the possibility of her loss. Meltzer understood life as a quest to sustain an apprehension of beauty that 'contains in its very nature the apprehension of the possibility of its destruction' (1988, p. 6). These groups for very frail older people and their carers embodied such a quest and capture the tension in trying to help them and their carers sustain a love of the beauty of life whilst suffering the pain of its ending.

# PART II
# INDIRECT THERAPEUTIC
# CONSULTATIONS

# 7

# Ageist Attitudes and Behaviours

## Introduction

When Freud was 48 years old he made the notorious pronouncement that 'near or above the age of fifty the elasticity of mental processes, on which the (psychoanalytic) treatment depends, is as a rule lacking' (Freud, 1905b, p. 264). Freud's ageism is especially poignant because he himself demonstrated an extraordinary mental agility in his capacity to continue to revise and develop his theories until he died in his eighties. Nearly a hundred years after Freud's pronouncement, despite a growing body of successful therapeutic work with older people, a survey in 2003 of trainee clinical psychologists' attitudes about working with older people found that many of the trainees were as pessimistic as Freud. Some of the trainees thought they were influenced by older people's own views that they were 'too old to change', and by cultural assumptions like you can't teach 'old dogs new tricks'. Even those trainees who considered older people might be able to change, thought it was nonetheless 'pointless because there's little time left to benefit' and 'ultimately they're going to die' (Lee et al, 2003).

More recently there are accounts in the UK of older people going into hospital for routine surgery ending up malnourished, unkempt and left to die (Morrison, 2006). The journalist reporting these incidents speculated that the 'logic' nurses might use in justifying such neglect is that the old people are 'going to die anyway'. We are of course all going to die anyway but this logic reflects the defence of projective identification in which in the mind of the younger nurse or journalist or the trainee clinical psychologist, fears of death are disowned and projected into the older person. Certainly leaving the older patients starving and neglected ensured that they would fear for their survival. There are many perspectives about ageism but in this chapter I intend to examine unconscious aspects of ageism in projective identification, particularly the underlying terrors which propel the use of this defence mechanism.

Projective identification is not a one-way process and I shall also examine reciprocal projective processes which support ageism. For example in a psychotherapy group for older people, a woman in her seventies said to one of the therapists, in a mocking tone of voice, 'When are you going to stop growing!' (Personal Communication, Mark Ardern). The therapist was then in his mid-forties, feeling somewhat inexperienced as a group therapist and rather helpless in relation to a group which seemed to show little development. When the older woman addressed him in this way he felt put on the spot and uncertain how to respond. The older woman, who had difficulty using the therapy group to change, had projected capacities for development into the therapist which were expressed concretely as if he were still physically growing. At the same time she mocked such capacities by infantilising the therapist. This could be seen as a form of envy of the therapist's comparative youth but the envious attack on the therapist's capacities was fuelled by the older woman projecting her own capacities for development into the therapist. She thereby felt herself depleted of such capacities and was then angry because they seemed to reside only in the younger therapist (see Symington, 2001, p. 49 for this understanding of the projective process underlying envy). This attack contributed to the therapist's sense of helplessness. Thus the mocking infantilisation is an attempt to disown dependency and effectively projects unwanted helplessness into the therapist.

## The projection of core fears of ageing: dependency, loneliness and death

Ageist projections may be only loosely connected to the chronological age of the recipients, or indeed their physical or mental states. Nonetheless there are certain realities connected with ageing which give some realistic hooks for these projections. In old age as the body shows undeniable signs of wearing out we are more than likely to become dependent again on others to care for us, our social world shrinks as our contemporaries die and we face the inevitability of our own demise. The terrors that are split off and projected in ageist attitudes are connected with core fears about the realities of growing old, namely dependency, loneliness and death (Terry, 2006). I shall discuss examples of each of these fears with illustrations of reciprocal projective identifications and the underlying terrors which fuel the projective processes.

## Dependency

*Fears of dependency can be projected between therapist or carer and older person, particularly in infantilising attitudes and behaviour. Such fears may reflect problems in the dependency relationship in infancy or child-hood when the infant was not sufficiently held and exposed to terrors of unintegration.*

It might be wondered why the older woman in the group would want to disown and mock capacities for growth and development. When she divested herself of her own developmental capacities, projected them into her middle-aged therapist and mocked him as a young boy still growing, she confirmed a view that the therapist was not to be depended upon. After all what could he, so young and inexperienced, offer to old people? This was then a way of avoiding any possible dependency on the therapist and of rendering him helpless which confirmed his uselessness.

The projection of dependency works both ways. For example a psychoanalyst, writing of his experiences with an older client, describes receiving a phone call from a 65 year-old woman enquiring about a vacancy for psychoanalytic treatment. She made a strong and forceful impression on the analyst. He then found himself very carefully giving her instructions about how to find his consulting room as though 'she were a helpless old lady who had to be told everything twice because of her age' (Hinze, 1987, p. 472). He later reflected on the unconscious counter-transference process and concluded he was driven by a need not to feel small and helpless when faced with an older woman who could remind him of a powerful mother. In other words, because of his ability to reflect on his unconscious he realised that he was pro-jecting helplessness into this older woman out of a fear of infantile dependency.

A dread of dependency is perhaps most conspicuous in worries about the consequences of suffering illnesses like a stroke or dementia. I shall now quote an excerpt from an observational study by a clinical psychology trainee of a day-room of a dementia unit (Chapter 10 gives further information about these observational studies):

*There are several older people seated in the day-room. Apart from the observer no staff are present. One woman says 'Someone has stolen my tin of biscuits and we all know who it is!' She stares at one of the other women who remains silent and seems unresponsive. One of the men, Mr Hart is wearing a suit and tie. A carer comes in and says 'Take your coat off Bill it's too warm in here'. The carer leaves.*

*Mr Hart then looks at a book of crossword puzzles and says nothing. His wife who is visiting sits alongside him and says crossly to him 'Where is the pen? I'm not going to give you another pen if you're going to lose them!' Another woman, Mrs Reed, who seemed to be sleeping, opens her eyes and smiles at the observer saying 'No more pens'. A different carer comes in and gives Mrs Reed a cup of tea telling her not to spill it. Mrs Reed tries to put the cup and saucer on the floor. The carer tells her where to put it. The carer leaves. Mr Hart's wife tells him to drink his tea.*

These older people who are suffering from dementia are undoubtedly struggling with losses which they express through the lost tin of biscuits and the lost pens. They are painfully losing their independence and losing their minds. However, the carers and the visiting wife contribute to these losses by infantilising these old people. Treating them as children is projecting dependency into them and effectively stealing any remaining independent capacities for thought or action that these people may have left. It is as though only the carers or the visiting relative have any independent capacities.

An excerpt from a later observation of this day-room in the dementia unit illustrates the force of the projective process in which unconsciously the carers need to discourage their clients' attempts at independence and instead ensure a humiliating infantile dependency:

*Mrs Reed tries to get up out of her chair. The observer feels frightened she will fall. Mrs Reed flops down in her chair. Later she tries to get up again. She manages to stand up just when a carer comes in and says 'Sit down Eileen, you'll break your back!' Mrs Reed sits immediately. The observer is shocked. The carer leaves. Mrs Reed tries again. This time the observer feels like urging her on and wants to say 'Come on you can do it'. Another carer comes in and says to Mrs Reed 'Sit down or you'll fall'. Once again Mrs Reed tries. The carer says impatiently 'Sit down! What's the matter with you!', and then looking more closely, as though talking to a naughty child, 'Oh you've gotten yourself wet!' The carer brings a wheel chair and takes Mrs Reed away.*

Consciously the carers are trying to look after these old people as best they can and they are probably frightened, like the observer, that the old people might injure themselves by falling. Consciously or unconsciously, the carers are terrified of the mental and physical disintegration they behold in those they care for, terrified of the spectre of helplessness these old people conjure for the carers' own old age.

I think the carers are also recipients of projected fears from their dementing clients who struggle with the terror of their minds falling to pieces or breaking apart. However the carers' own terrors and those they receive from their clients are projected back into someone like Mrs Reed when she is told she'll break her back. The carers are helpless to stop Mrs Reed's disintegration but at the same time unconsciously they ensure the helplessness resides in Mrs Reed who, despite her attempts to assert her dignity and independence, is reduced to a helpless incontinent infant.

Psychoanalytic studies have revealed how fears of dependency have their origins in infancy. Fears of dependency and the underlying terrors of unintegration are also discussed in Chapter 3 in relation to the therapy with Mrs Taylor 'who collapsed into helplessness'. Brian Martindale's work shows how older people become fearful about becoming 'dependent again' when there have been failures in the early dependency relationship in childhood. Ageing and the anticipation or experience of dependency because of the decline in physical or mental capacities, bring fears that again dependency needs will not be met. Martindale writes of how such worries can be projectively communicated to younger therapists who then dread the older client becoming dependent on them. Such worries may be exacerbated for the therapist if he or she is also faced with the dependency needs of his or her ageing parents (Martindale, 1989a).

Observational studies of infants and their mothers have revealed that underlying the fears of dependency and helplessness are infantile terrors of unintegration from experiences of being unheld. At first the infant needs the mother, or primary caretaker, to bind the different parts of its personality together, by physically holding and mentally holding the infant in mind. If there are sufficient good enough experiences of holding then eventually the infant and child internalise this holding capacity for him- or herself, which is experienced like the skin holding the body together (Bick, 1968). Prolonged experiences of being unheld expose the infant to catastrophic anxieties of 'unintegration', of 'falling to pieces or dissolving into space' (Symington, 1985). Analytic work with children and adults shows how, when there have been problems of holding, the infant and child develop premature ways of holding him- or herself together which can become entrenched defences against dependency, covering over the underlying dread of unintegration. However, experiences which revive infantile helplessness 'bring back echoes of that very early unheld precariousness' (Symington, 1985, p. 486). This work signals ubiquitous underlying terrors associated with dependency. Most if not all infant experiences will include ordinary lapses in maternal care when the baby may be unheld and exposed to the terrors of falling to pieces. Such experiences leave a residual terror, in 'pockets of disturbance' (Garland, 1991) in the unconscious. These terrors can be revived with the anticipation or experience of dependency and helplessness, and contribute to the pressure to split off and project these states of mind in ageist attitudes and behaviour. Moreover, because projective identification can be used in phantasy to possess and control, these projective processes and terrors may underlie 'King Lear' attitudes of tyranny and control in older people or their carers (Hess, 1987).

## Loneliness

*Fears of loneliness are often accompanied by feelings of shame which come from a severe self-critical force or super-ego which also discourages dependency and insists on perfection. Older people can be particularly vulnerable to these projected fears when they are segregated in institutions and understandably feel rejected and unwanted.*

Noel Hess who is a clinical psychologist and psychoanalytic psychotherapist has written about understanding the experience of loneliness in old age and the shame and humiliation that is often associated with loneliness. Hess gives a clinical vignette from a time when, although experienced as a clinical psychologist, he had just started working with older people. He writes of a 65 year-old woman who was referred to him for psychotherapy. From the first phone call this woman made it clear she felt it was an insult to be referred to someone so young and inexperienced. When they met she continued to complain about his youth, insensitivity and incompetence. She had a long history of depression and had herself worked in the helping profession. Hess was able to make some contact with this woman particularly when he was able to understand how very lonely she felt. She told him that she was now suffering from a degenerative condition which would worsen as she aged. However, she attended for just two interviews. She felt it was impossible to continue because of the age gap and asked her doctor to be referred to someone else (Hess, 2004).

Hess felt thrown by the force of this woman's criticisms, and helpless about how to engage her in therapy. This woman projected helplessness that comes from inexperience and youth or infancy into him, and at the same time was very contemptuous of such feelings. Of course he did lack experience in working with older people, and it is in the nature of this projective defence that it finds real aspects of the recipients with which to mobilise the projected feelings. The task for the therapist is to disentangle what belongs to him or her that facilitates the projection, from what belongs to the client and needs to be understood.

It is particularly the force of condemnation which is associated with the projection that sheds some light on why this woman may have found the degenerative condition particularly difficult because in her mind helplessness and dependency were so held in contempt. The condemnation and contempt are understood as coming from a critical agency or force in the unconscious mind, sometimes described in the psychoanalytic literature as an 'abnormal' (O'Shaughnessy, 1999) or 'implacable' (Mason, 1981) super-ego, in contrast to a more usual and benign super-ego or conscience. Such a harsh super-ego can be seen in the earlier example underneath the older woman's mockery of her group therapist's youth. It is this implacable super-ego that intensifies the experience of loneliness, on the one hand by condemning dependence on anyone and on the other hand by constructing an idealised view of a relationship in which there would be perfect unity and understanding. The condemnation of dependency means that relationships are diminished or avoided. The idealisation leads to a painful longing for an unattainable ideal and makes a persecuting demand for perfection in oneself or another. The result can be a dreadful stigma and shame about loneliness which comes from the internal criticisms for wanting an intimate relationship and for not being perfect enough to achieve one.

Older people are naturally more vulnerable to loneliness because as they age fewer and fewer of their contemporaries will survive, or because of the problems of mobility and keeping in touch. There is a particular terror of dying alone or of dying with terrible experiences in one's head which have never been discussed with anyone else. The loneliness is often reinforced by the segregation of the old into ghettoes in contemporary western society, whether for example in retirement villages or dementia wards. In the wards and nursing homes it is commonplace for the staff to remain quite separate, often very convivial with one another, but having little interaction with the older people. In such settings there is also little contact between the residents, who typically sit silently around the walls of a day-room with a television that no one watches. There are of course many reasons for this segregation, but I think an important unconscious motive, either in staff or their older clients, is to lodge into those whom they regard as old the terror of a loneliness that foreshadows death. For example in the previous chapter I have described group meetings in which older people or staff mocked the isolated, cut off monologues of other members of the group whom they described as 'poor old dears'. Again such projections can find realistic hooks in the older people because of internal self-criticisms and self-denigration, such as views that they are not worth bothering with, and no-one wants them.

## Death

*Fears of death and dying are linked to fears of dependency. Fears of death can create particular problems in the counter-transference and lead to difficulties in the ending of therapy with older people. The therapist's capacity to reflect on his or her fears of death can prevent diminishing the therapeutic opportunities for older people and may lead to important developments in the therapy.*

Brian Martindale writes of how many older clients say they do not fear death but they are afraid of dying. Martindale links the fear of dying with failures in the early dependency relationship. The dread of suffering a lingering death, being helpless and vulnerable comes from the fear that once again there will be a failure to receive dependable love and care (2007). Elliott Jaques describes the contradictory views between Freud who maintained that the unconscious has no awareness of death, and Klein who held there was an unconscious awareness of death. Jaques sees this as only an apparent contradiction because whilst he agrees 'the unconscious is not aware of death per se', he says 'there are unconscious experiences akin to those which later appear in consciousness as notions of death' (1965, p. 236). He illustrates such experiences with a dream I described in the previous chapter in which death is portrayed as a state of being immobilised and mute but able to experience everything. Perhaps this image holds particular terror because the fear of dying and fear of death are conflated in this unconscious experience of death.

As discussed in Chapter 1, Franco De Masi (2004) has pointed out that even in such frightening unconscious images of death the self is still present: what is unimaginable is *nothingness* and death is therefore an 'excessive trauma for the mind'. De Masi concludes that what is especially terrifying is the destruction of civilisation. Thus, I believe the unconscious terrors of death have intensified in more recent times because of the amassing of enough weapons of nuclear destruction to destroy our entire civilisation. Perhaps then it is not so surprising that in the west where these weapons have proliferated there is an ever increasing intolerance of those who are old and who bring dreadful reminders of vulnerability and death. Despite the forecasts of increasing numbers of older people provision of care for the old in the UK is more and more reduced or dismantled, often transferred from the National Health Service to a cost-cutting and exploitative private sector (Terry, 1998).

Such ageism extends not only to the care of severely ill old people but also to the provision of counselling and psychotherapy. It seems that not only do many clinical psychology trainees think there is no point in offering therapy to older people, but many GPs hold similar views despite the research evidence of the effectiveness of psychotherapy for older people (Davenhill, 2007a, p. 21). A recent paper surveying work reported in the USA in two 'premier counselling' journals over the last ten years reveals a conspicuous paucity of any accounts of work with older people (Werth et al, 2003). The British Association for Counselling and Psychotherapy journal *Therapy Today*, which devoted a special issue in 2006 to older clients, noted in its editorial, with some embarrassment, that it had been five years since there had been any substantial report of work with older clients.

Within the therapeutic work that is offered ageism can impede the therapeutic process. A study of some psychoanalysts, who had experience of working with older people, reveals particular problems arising from the analyst's unconscious attitudes reflected in the counter-transference which were especially connected with fears of death. For example a common difficulty was reported in handling problems of termination of the analysis because of the analysts' ambivalences and hesitations, which were understood as connected with the lack of other people in the older client's life and the end of the analysis presaging the death of the older client. Sometimes arrangements were made for intermittent contact following the formal ending of the analysis (Plotkin, 2000). Recommending the spacing out intervals between the sessions when approaching termination with older clients (for example Reggiori, 2004) may reflect similar difficulties. The central difficulty the analysts identified was sorting out the reality of the implications of decline, illness and medical crisis from the analysts' unconscious fears.

One author of a research study involving interviews with therapists working with older people concluded:

'a response to these feelings (of seeing the future of loss and death) that I believe came through the interviews and in my own reflections, ...is to be much more easily caught up in the client's stories about the past and an inclination to be gentler and more flexible with boundaries. I find it much harder not to answer direct questions, such as whether I have a family, from an older client.' (Atkins and Loewenthal, 2004, p. 508)

I can readily identify with these difficulties in my own work with older and sometimes infirm clients. I struggle with questions of whether to pursue a supportive approach or whether a firm analytic stance, and struggle too with issues about boundaries and termination. To paraphrase a question raised in the report of the analysts' work: the difficult dilemma to sort out is whether my worries about the client's durability are screening worries about *my* durability. In essence when I decide on a supportive approach, or put off making a termination date, am I projecting terrors of death into the client? In other words am I treating the client as if he or she is too near or too frightened of death, or too vulnerable for a robust interpretative approach or for an definite ending to be faced?

Reciprocally there are other studies which show how older clients may identify with ageism, project into their therapist's fears and thereby diminish the therapy. For example, in an account of work with an older woman her younger analyst felt tempted to accept the woman's complaint of 'stress incontinence' as simply a symptom of old age. But resisting this temptation the analyst instead explored the unconscious meaning of the incontinence which led to important insights about the woman's conflicts about her sexuality. At another time this woman wanted to finish the analysis because of practical problems connected with her retirement. The analyst was tempted to go along with the request to end. Instead by withstanding the pressure to project fears of ageing and death into the client, and by reflecting on these fears the analyst was able to help his client pursue the analytic work. The client's unconscious fears about going further in the analysis were then revealed and led to important developments in the therapeutic work (Wylie, 1987).

## Summary

Understanding the unconscious aspects of ageism in projective identifications between older people and their carers or therapists, illuminates the interactive nature of this prejudice in the reciprocal projections that reinforce it. Core fears of dependency, loneliness and death are projected back and forth in ageist attitudes and behaviour, because of underlying terrors which are felt to be unmanageable and which are shared by us all. A central terror is an infantile dread of unintegration, which is described as fears of falling to pieces and which underlies fears of dependency. Early experiences of unintegration are the first glimpses of the terrifying nothingness of death. Hence the terrors associated with dependency and death may have their origin in a dread of unintegration from experiences of being unheld in infancy.

To manage a dread of unintegration the infant develops ways of holding him- or herself together such as through a physical or mental muscularity. Albert Mason proposes that the infant manages these terrors by creating the phantasy of an omnipotent internal agency, an implacable super-ego born of the 'implacable phantasies of the helpless infant' (1981). Alternatively, Bion (1959) describes how the absent, uncontaining mother becomes an inner presence which he described as an 'ego destructive super-ego'. Such an agency in the mind may be a punitive and ruthless super-ego but it is thereby a steely force with which to hold oneself together against terrors of unintegration. Furthermore it is intolerant of and discourages dependency but also insists on unattainable ideals for a perfect partner. It is relentless in its demands for perfection, and contributes to the humiliation of dependency and the shame of loneliness. The omnipotence of this super-ego provides protection against the reality of death by supporting phantasies of immortality. Elliott Jaques has pointed out such protection comes at a high price because omnipotent demands for perfection are inevitably persecuting (1965).

The operation of such a super-ego can be seen in the bipolarity and persecutory demands of contemporary images of ageing, implicit in the promotion of 'successful ageing' or 'agelessness' alongside the shadow of 'decline and death' (McHugh, 2003). In other words the very agency that is created to manage terrors of unintegration and death itself becomes terrifying, a reflection of what Freud recognised as a 'return of the repressed' (1896). These underlying terrors are revived through the experience of ageing or contact with those who are old and becoming dependent again, more vulnerable to loneliness and nearer to death. Such terrors are evacuated in ageist attitudes and behaviour, and hook into the painful realities of growing old.

Projective identification is used not only to rid oneself of such frightening feelings but lodging parts of the self in someone else is in unconscious phantasy a way of possessing and controlling the other. Furthermore, treating the other as an extension of oneself denies separateness. So, although there is an attempt to disown fears of dependency, loneliness and death, this projective defence tries to ensure that there is someone who can be controlled and is therefore dependable, and tries to avoid the experience of real separateness by projectively gluing oneself to another.

Projective identification is understood as our earliest means of communication by evoking feelings in mother or primary carer as a means of being understood and of ultimately being able to understand. It is a form of communication to which we need resort throughout life especially for unmanageable feelings and experiences which test our limits and go beyond words. In therapy as in motherhood the task is to be receptive to and manage the projections without forcing them back undigested, to engage in a 'reverie' to try to understand what is being communicated, to find words to promote thought and understanding and eventually enable the projections to be retrieved and integrated into the self. Such opportunities for containment, for support and reflection were doubtless non-existent for the overstretched nursing staff on the ward (where the older woman was left to die) and were absent too for the carers on the dementia unit. The result is that the projected fears of the older person remain unprocessed and are returned to him or her with the likely addition of terrors belonging to the carer or nurse. Moreover, because this defence is not simply a passive phantasy, the projection can have debilitating consequences whereby the phantasy in the projection is enacted, ensuring that the older person will fear for his or her life or be entrenched in a state of infantile dependency.

In contrast when the older woman patient wanted to bring her therapy to a premature end, under the guise of issues about retirement, her therapist was able to disentangle her projected terrors of ageing and death from his own terrors. This central therapeutic element of containment meant that the therapist did not reproject his client's terrors mixed up with his own, but instead he was able to help her to better understand and work through her worries about pursuing therapy, which had galvanised around fears about retirement and death. It is an example of how the processing of projected terrors associated with ageing can ameliorate the debilitating consequences of ageism. It also demonstrates the value and importance of providing a reflective space for those who are involved in care with older people.

The processing of projective identifications is extremely complex because these are essentially unconscious and the projections often hook into real aspects of the recipient of the projections. Therapists, carers or relatives will need the support of a third figure if they are to maintain a receptiveness to the emotional and wordless states of those for whom they care, to maintain a capacity not to be overwhelmed and to sort out what is projected into them. The disentangling of one's own fears from those projected by another is provided by a third perspective which for the therapist may come from a clinical supervisor, or an internalised supervisor in the therapist's mind or a body of theory, knowledge and understanding (Caper, 1999). For carers and relatives of those who are old, containment means providing a time and a place for reflection, preferably with someone removed from the emotional turmoil of the day-to-day care, and who can think about the terrors underlying the projective identifications in ageist attitudes and behaviour.

# 8

# INDIVIDUAL CONSULTATIONS
# WITH CARERS

## Introduction

As part of 'good practice' and 'person-centred care' it is usual in hospitals or residential settings for patients or residents to be assigned to a particular carer, variously described with titles such as the 'named nurse' or 'keyworker' or 'case manager'. In this chapter I shall use the term keyworker. The keyworkers are responsible for their patient(s), especially getting to know the patient and whenever possible working with the patient to provide some continuity of care. When older people in long stay care were referred to me I found it important to meet with the keyworker. These consultations can provide useful information about the referral. Quite often the consultations support the keyworker in working therapeutically with his or her patient with the result that there is no need for a direct psychotherapeutic intervention. Chapter 6 gives a description of the long stay care setting and the care staff and patients for whom I offered these consultations.

The aim in such consultations is to offer support to the keyworkers by giving some time and space for them to talk about their own feelings, and by helping them understand that some of the feelings they experience could be unconscious communications from their patients. Hence their feelings may help them gain a better understanding of the emotional experiences of their older patients. This consultative support could be offered by an experienced and possibly more senior colleague to carers, whether carers are staff or family. Carers have to bear the physical and emotional strain of close contact with ill and damaged and sometimes angry and provocative patients. I took an interest in the carers' work and encouraged them to talk about and reflect on their own feelings; and think about their patients' feelings, by following my example and imaginatively putting themselves in their patients' shoes. I tried to help them understand how it felt to be that patient in long stay care. Jane Garner, writing of staff in dementia care says: 'Staff need the freedom to recognise negative as well as positive feelings and the freedom to say these things in order to remain able to use their personal and professional skills for their patients' (2004, p. 223).

This consultative work challenges a defensive process in caring organisations in which staff can often become mindless and unable to think about their patients' feelings, in order to protect themselves from the pain of empathising with their patients' emotional states; and perhaps in order to protect the institution from a more mindful, and therefore perhaps more critical staff (Dartington, 1994). As I indicated earlier in Chapter 2, in the role of the psychologist I may be a recipient for staff's capacity to think about patients' feelings which can be split off and located in me as the 'expert'. Working with the keyworkers was one way of repairing the split by showing staff that with support it is possible for them to bear to think and to feel with their patients. Though thinking in this way can make the work more painful, ultimately it can be more fulfilling of the reparative wishes that bring staff to this work.

The consultations also illustrates the danger that when staff have no opportunity to talk about and understand their own feelings or their patients', then not thinking can easily lead to retaliatory and abusive practices. The consultations with keyworkers brought to light some instances of abusive treatment of patients. In research about abuse there has been difficulty reaching agreement about definitions of abuse and methodologies (Glendenning, 1993). What has become clear is the importance of the caregiving relationship because it is recognised that abuse, whether in an institutional or domestic setting, 'exists within the context of a relationship and represents a caregiving relationship gone awry' (Phillips, quoted by Nolan, 1993, p. 150). Nolan has emphasised that in order to prevent abuse we need to understand more about the caregiving relationship, particularly to see it as a dynamic and changing relationship; to recognise that it is not simply concerned with the physical care but also involves the emotional needs of older patient and carer; and to appreciate that in the caregiving role, alongside its stresses, there are rewards and satisfactions (Nolan, 1993). The consultations with keyworkers which I shall describe address Nolan's points by providing an opportunity to gain more understanding about the caregiving relationship, whether in institutions or domestic settings, and a place where instances of abuse can be addressed. Moreover the consultations contribute to the prevention of abuse by offering containment for the difficulties and acknowledgement of the satisfactions in the caring role.

In this chapter and the next when working with the carers I adopted the carer's use of the patient's first name. I am uncomfortable with too quick a familiarity, particularly for a generation accustomed to more formality, but unlike the carers I was not involved in the intimate physical contact necessary when looking after these frail old people.

## Recovery and despair – Barbara and Mrs Dulcie May

*These consultations meant keeping in mind the keyworker's and her patient's hope and despair. Discovering some meaning in her patient's behaviour enabled the keyworker to understand more about her experience with her patient and her own experience of ageing.*

Barbara was an enrolled nurse who had worked for many years in the hospital. She was a vivacious woman in her late fifties, full of life and good humour. I used to meet with her in the early evenings, sitting in the nurses' office looking out onto the ward. As I got to know Barbara I became impressed with her sensitivity. A touching tribute came from one of her patients, an Indian woman, who spoke no English, when she pointed to Barbara and said to her grandson 'She loves me!'

I was asked to see Dulcie May an 80 year-old woman who had been transferred from the rehabilitation ward to the long stay following a car accident which resulted in her losing her speech and memory. A speech therapist visited her regularly and found she could sometimes communicate by writing. She could walk with some assistance, could do a few tasks for herself, but was generally incapacitated by the accident and in a great deal of distress.

Barbara was Dulcie's keyworker. She told me Dulcie had been hit by a car when crossing the road with her husband who was uninjured. However, her husband suffered from dementia. Dulcie had been looking after him for several years. Following the accident her husband was admitted to a nursing home because there was no one else to look after him. Dulcie was asked if she wanted to join her husband in the nursing home. She seemed adamant against doing so, and wanted to live with her brother. Barbara told me Dulcie was beginning to recover her memory, but then kept forgetting where she was. Apparently she had been actively involved in the local community. She used to go out each day to various luncheons. Barbara was full of admiration for the way Dulcie struggled to speak and remember. Barbara said Dulcie used to cry whenever any of her visitors left her. Recently she had screamed at lunchtime on the activities ward. I talked to Barbara about Dulcie's shock and pain at awakening to her disabled state. Instead of being at a social luncheon she found herself surrounded by disabled old people.

The following week when I saw Barbara she told me Dulcie wrote that she was lonely. But when they took her to the day-room, after briefly acknowledging the other patients, she wanted to be taken back to her bed. I said I thought it was unbearable to be reminded of her incapacitated state by seeing other patients who were like a reflection of herself. Barbara said she had a similar thought when she noticed Dulcie preferred being with the staff. She went on to say that Dulcie seemed only to want to live in the present. She mostly wrote 'hungry' asking for food, or 'tired' when she wanted to be put to bed. It was unclear whether she had any recall of the accident. She showed little interest in the past or future. I said I felt the accident had been a brush with death. A lively and vigorous woman had been confronted with her ageing and vulnerability. Barbara blushed as she recalled an incident with her own adolescent son when he objected to the clothes she was wearing, saying she looked like a teenager. She had been angry with him, but in telling me she poignantly saw difficulties in facing her own ageing.

We talked some more about Dulcie's distress about her age catching up with her. Barbara said she usually found that it was more difficult for the male patients to accept what had happened to them. I recalled that Dulcie had been the head of the household for some years, caring for an increasingly dependent husband. Following his dementia he had little memory, and now Dulcie felt like him and only had a present. I thought the disability around her would remind her of her husband's incapacities and her fears for him and herself.

The next week Dulcie seemed to be speaking more. She was livelier and had been going to the activities ward. She'd conveyed to Barbara that her family hadn't wanted her to marry her husband, there was some feeling he wasn't good enough for her. It seemed even now her family were objecting to her going to live with him at the nursing home. But her husband was regularly brought to see her. Sometimes he seemed not to recognise her, though when it was time for him to leave they both cried.

Two weeks later Dulcie had become withdrawn and depressed again. Barbara said she only spoke when spoken to, and only looked forward to going to bed. Barbara was keen to move her to the more stimulating environment of a nursing home. I said I felt Dulcie was probably despairing because as she made some progress she would also realise that however much she improved she would never be the same as before. I thought Dulcie might feel life wasn't worth living any more. Barbara said one of the doctors had suggested Dulcie might be able to return home but she thought that most unlikely. I said it was difficult to hold onto the hope and the sadness, without exaggerating what might be possible and without being overwhelmed by despair. Then Barbara said she found it difficult to talk to Dulcie, particularly because Dulcie didn't seem to want to talk about her past. I said it was important to talk to Dulcie about her present disappointments and fears about the future, in the wake of her disabilities. Barbara replied that everything was getting her down. She talked about problems with other staff on the ward. She had tried to introduce various changes in the keyworker system but she felt the staff were jealous of her; and there was rivalry about who could do the various jobs on the ward. I said the rivalry amongst the staff avoided facing their despair about what couldn't be done for these very ill and damaged patients, and avoided taking in the patients' despair about what they could no longer do for themselves.

For the next few weeks there was some excitement as Dulcie continued to make progress. She regained a good deal of her former capacities. Her memory recovered and she was able to speak again, though she remained frail and in need of supervised care. There was a struggle between members of Dulcie's family, herself and Barbara, about whether she would go to live in the nursing home with her husband, go to a separate nursing home, or remain as a long stay patient on the ward. Barbara was keen for her to be reunited with her husband. I said that perhaps they didn't want to be with each other. They might be glad to live separately. Barbara seemed to have a vision of them walking off hand in hand into the sunset. Barbara laughed as I said this. She was deeply shocked to see how strongly she felt that they should be together, and how this obstructed her from discovering just what it was that Dulcie wanted.

Two months later Dulcie and her husband were given a trial period of living together at the nursing home. In the time preparing for the move Barbara gradually drew back a little from Dulcie, and was less insistent that Dulcie and her husband should remain together. As it turned out the trial period was successful and they stayed together in the nursing home.

## Commentary

My taking up the referrals, like Dulcie, by offering consultations with the keyworkers was accepted by the staff, because it was seen to be helpful. Barbara was generous in telling other staff about her appreciation of this work. She said she was helped to think and become more aware of her patient's feelings. Perhaps it was the meeting in the early evenings, but sometimes I thought of my role in relation to Barbara, like a husband who comes home and hears about the day's troubles – particularly problems with the children – and thereby offers some support by thinking about his wife's worries. I felt I was able to help Barbara make some sense of Dulcie's behaviour, like the screaming and her reluctance to mix with the other patients. Barbara came to understand that feelings stirred in her could be a communication of how her patient felt. It seemed especially important to help Barbara keep in mind Dulcie's grief, and resist the urge to provide a busy programme in which there would be no space for sad feelings. At the same time, the hope that Dulcie could recover needed acknowledging, together with the disappointment that she might not recover as everyone wished. These attitudes were quite split, sometimes being expressed in exaggerated ways in different staff, like the doctor's hope that Dulcie would be able to return home, alongside Barbara's feeling of despair. The argument about whether or not Dulcie should live with her husband in a nursing home included a similar split, as though if she lived separately she would not be contaminated by any disability; or that if they lived together they could be reunited as a wholesome, happy couple. I aimed to help Barbara achieve a more realistic view of Dulcie's future, and to be less driven to impose her own happy ending on a tragedy. I felt if she could help Dulcie grieve about what had happened, then Dulcie might be able to make the most of what remained of her life.

## A persecuting grief – Melody and Mrs Ruth Scott

*When it was possible to think about the patient's feelings of loss, and to give space for some of the keyworker's personal bereavement, the keyworker did not feel so persecuted by her patient's feelings. There was then some opportunity for sad and appreciative feelings to be shared between the keyworker and her patient.*

Melody, an Afro-Caribbean staff nurse, was in her late twenties. She worked on the same ward as Barbara, who suggested Melody see me about her patient, Ruth Scott. Melody told me Ruth was 89 years old. She had married for the first time when she was 72. Twelve years later she became ill with Parkinson's Disease. Her husband had looked after her until he died, five months ago, when she was admitted to hospital.

Melody said she kept feeling irritated with Ruth because she was always making a strange 'mewing' noise. Melody asked me 'Why does she do that?' I could see she felt quite tormented by Ruth's mewing. When I asked her to describe the mewing, she 'mewed' like Ruth in a way that made me think of a cat's miaow. So I said maybe Ruth was calling for her cat. Perhaps along with so much that she had lost, including a husband whom she had married so late in life, she had also lost her cat. Melody softened as she heard these comments. Then, more sympathetically, she told me how Ruth often withdrew into herself, cried and curled up in bed. Sometimes she mentioned having dreams to Melody, but she did not say what the dreams were about. I said perhaps she dreamt of all that she missed. I felt she was consumed with grief. Melody became sad. She told me of her uncle who had recently died.

The next week Melody greeted me with obvious pleasure, immediately telling me indeed Ruth had had a cat! Melody had asked her about her life and her husband. Ruth told Melody her husband's name, but she seemed puzzled by Melody's interest. She said 'What's it got to do with you?' However, during the week Ruth had gone to Bingo and seemed to have enjoyed it. Melody was pleased. I felt Melody wanted Ruth to be active and enjoying herself. I reminded her that Ruth needed some space to grieve all that she had lost. She then asked me what other information she could find out about Ruth. I encouraged her to simply see what Ruth wanted to talk about, just to follow her conversation. Perhaps Melody could tell her a bit about herself and her own life. Again Melody asked me 'Why does Ruth mew then?' I said I thought she was calling to her lost cat, her lost husband, and perhaps even the children she never had.

The next two weeks Melody told me that Ruth called out in a distressed state much of the time. I said she might feel in a panic that everyone would disappear from her life. She could feel she herself might die at any time. I suggested that Melody reminded her of a daughter or grand-daughter she never had and who would perhaps have looked after her now. Melody said she'd asked Ruth about children. Ruth told her how much she'd have liked to have had a daughter. Melody looked sorrowful as she told me this.

Two weeks later, Melody said that Ruth was constantly calling out 'Help, help!' They couldn't discover what it was she wanted or what frightened her. She had spoken to Melody about having 'regrets' but did not say more, other than a confusing comment that she had 'impersonated someone'. In a quieter moment she said she liked the red T-shirt Melody wore, it was her favourite colour. I said I thought she was telling Melody how she appreciated her loving care, which reminded her of other good experiences in her life. Ruth had mentioned her mother and again a sense of regret, but would say no more. Melody remarked how different Ruth was now because she was talking more to her. Then Melody told me she was to be away for the next few weeks. I encouraged her to tell Ruth, to say for how long she'd be away and when she'd be back. I reminded Melody how important she was to Ruth, especially now that Ruth had begun talking. It was probably a huge relief for Ruth to talk, because it would be so awful to die with a lot of bad stuff inside her head. Several weeks later Ruth died. I had a final meeting with Melody to talk about her feelings about losing Ruth.

## Commentary

I felt that Ruth was grief-stricken and probably felt angry and tormented by her losses, especially the loss of a husband after a late and short-lived marriage. It seemed some of this state of mind had been conveyed to Melody when she felt irritated by the mewing and puzzled about its meaning, which may also have captured some of Ruth's torment and difficulty in finding a meaning in her own life. Melody was clearly relieved to gain some understanding of Ruth's behaviour.

I had a reciprocal difficulty in understanding Melody because of her accent. Sometimes I could not understand even after I'd asked her to repeat herself several times. As I think about this now, perhaps she was vividly conveying to me her frustration without being able to make sense of her patient. I wonder too if Ruth had difficulty in understanding Melody and how, Ruth, who was white, felt about having a black nurse caring for her. But these were not questions I felt I could put to Melody because of my own difficulty in addressing the meaning of race and difference in this work. In retrospect, I wish I had been able to tackle these questions head on, because not doing so diminished Melody and our opportunity to understand more about her work.

Melody probably found Ruth's grieving particularly difficult because Melody was suffering her own bereaved feelings about her uncle. As with Barbara, there was an intolerance of sad feelings and a wish to urge the patient into activities like the Bingo sessions. When I showed I could bear to think of Ruth's misery, Melody began to do so too. She recalled more of Ruth's distress, could feel sad for her and be in touch with her own sad feelings. Finding some meaning in Ruth's mewing and some understanding of her feelings led to some warm contact between Ruth and Melody, evident for example in the compliments about the red T-shirt. At those times I think Ruth felt more in touch with loving external and internal figures, and less consumed by persecutory feelings.

# Aggressive behaviour and abuse – Betty and Mr Arthur Green

*Thinking with the keyworker about her patient's aggressive behaviour enabled her to challenge some negative assumptions about him and abusive treatment by other carers.*

Betty had trained as an enrolled nurse but had not pursued a nursing career. Many years later she came to work in the hospital as an untrained care assistant. She was a somewhat bluff character, a rough cut diamond, warm and intuitive. When one of her patients was referred to me she was interested and pleased to consult me. Usually I talked to her in the office on the ward. Once when she came to my office she felt guilty about taking time off from the ward to see me. She said she should be working. I said 'But this *is* working!'

Arthur Green was 80 years old. He was admitted into long stay care just a few weeks before Christmas. Shortly after his admission he was referred to me because he had hit some care assistants on the ward. He suffered from Parkinson's Disease and cancer. Betty described Arthur as a 'bag of bones'. She said he tended to sit for most of the day with his eyes closed, except when she went to him. She used to joke with him asking 'Are you in or are you out?' Usually he would open his eyes and answer 'In!' At that time he was the only male patient on the ward. She said Arthur had not punched her but he could also be verbally abusive. She said she gave him 'as good as he gets' indicating she swore back at him when he swore at her. She discovered that he had a sweet tooth and quickly calmed down if she gave him a lolly or a cake. With sympathy she said he had been 'dumped' on the ward, with little preparation and no choice about whether he wanted to be there. His wife had been looking after him at home but was now no longer able to manage. Betty was concerned about his wife because she looked thin and undernourished, so she and the other staff always encouraged her to have some lunch with Arthur when she visited. Betty and the other staff believed Arthur had always been a violent man. They were surprised his wife visited regularly and seemed so close to him. I said I thought Arthur was bitter about what had happened to him, and terribly angry. I encouraged her to find out more about him.

Following a two-week Christmas break I saw Betty again, this time in my office. She had spoken with Arthur's daughter who told Betty that her father had only become violent late in life, after the onset of his illnesses. Previously he had been a kind, loving father and husband. As we talked Betty began to understand Arthur's violence as an

expression of his anger about his illnesses and the painful consequences, like the loss of his independence and now the loss of his home
and family life. Then Betty told me she was unhappy about the way
Arthur was being treated on the ward. Following his violent outbursts
he was removed from other patients who were in the day-room.
He was left in a chair alongside his bed at the other end of the ward, in
a draught. I talked to Betty about the cruelty in this way of treating
him. She thought they could instead place Arthur in the day-room out
of striking distance from other patients. At least he could then be with
the others and watch TV. I suggested Betty talk to her colleagues on the
ward, try to explain how Arthur felt and why he might be violent.

The next week Betty reported that Arthur had been taken to the day-
room. When some staff objected, apparently she told them: 'Well, Paul
Terry said "Why not give it a try?"'. Betty was still worried about him
and I agreed to have a meeting with her and Arthur together. She took
me to him to arrange it. I found a shrunken, emaciated man, hunched
in an armchair, his eyes closed. There seemed to be some secretion
around his eyes and Betty explained that he was suffering from an eye
infection. When I introduced myself he managed to open his eyes,
looked pleased about a meeting, and checked he had correctly understood the appointment time and day.

The day of the meeting Arthur's wife was visiting, so I suggested she
join us. She took over the meeting, insisting, in a nervous and guilty
way, that Arthur told us how happy he was here, how good the staff
were to him and how impossible it had been for her to manage. Arthur
complied and agreed with what his wife said, but he would not agree
that he was happy. As his wife talked on he gradually withdrew and
eventually fell asleep. Just before we were due to finish he woke. When
we arranged another meeting he warmly shook my hand. Betty's
change of shifts and holidays meant it was not possible for her to meet
with myself and Arthur for some time, so I met him on his own on two
more occasions. At these meetings he was confused and seemed to be
hallucinating, scarcely in touch with me or his surroundings. His condition worsened and he died shortly after.

## Commentary

Arthur's aggressive behaviour was understandably very hard for his
carers to manage. Without opportunities to reflect on the feelings provoked by such behaviour, the carers were vulnerable to acting out their
anger with him. The carers' fear, anger and physical hurt from such
behaviour can, if there is some reflective space, give some important

clues to the frightened, hurt and angry states that are being conveyed through a projective process because their patients may not have the words for or access to these feelings. Betty was verbally aggressive in response to Arthur but she could be encouraged to think about Arthur's feelings and her own. She was able to challenge her colleagues' negative assumptions about Arthur and their abusive treatment of him. The way Betty quoted me (with advice I don't recall giving) shows how important the relationship with me was in supporting her to address abusive behaviour.

I occasionally saw the keyworkers and their patients together. I offered to see Arthur with Betty because I was concerned to give Betty as much support as possible when she was faced with the other staff being abusive to Arthur. In the meeting with Arthur's wife it is apparent how difficult it can be for relatives to think about a patient's unhappiness or treatment on the ward. Relatives can feel guilty about no longer looking after the patient, and perhaps frightened that if they dared to complain, the patient would be sent back home.

Valerie Sinason (1988) has written of very subtle forms of abuse that can occur between mother and baby. For example she describes an observation of a mother bathing a young baby in which, when the mother first started wiping the baby's mouth, the baby showed signs of discomfort, which continued for some weeks though with less intensity. After just six weeks Sinason noticed the baby started smiling when the towel touched his mouth and the smiling continued. The mother and for a while Sinason too, believed that the baby was enjoying the wiping though Sinason began to feel that the mother had some uncomfortable appreciation of the aggressiveness in her behaviour. At six months the baby briefly showed some distress at the mother wiping his mouth sharply. A week later he was smiling again. In the context of a caregiving relationship Sinason's observations show how abusive behaviour can be covered over, in quite collusive ways 'to avoid unwelcome realisations' (1988) of abuse by the carer or by the patient.

Sinason points out how an infant is handled, in being dressed, undressed, cleaned or fed, 'can carry many disguised sadistic or erotic overtones'. So too with these older patients who, like infants, are also helpless, dependent and vulnerable to these subtle and not-so-subtle forms of abuse. Like Sinason's abused children, older patients can feel they have to 'swallow' the abuse. I heard of one carer who, prior to washing her patient used to strip her naked, leaving her cold and exposed. I was told of staff feeding patients by hand, engaged in conversations with each other and ignoring their patients.

One of Barbara's female patients, for whom my help was sought, upset the staff by smearing her faeces over her bed and surroundings. Barbara found it helpful when I gave some meaning to this repellent behaviour by comparing it to the protests prisoners had made in Northern Ireland. She said she'd never thought of the patients experiencing long stay care like a prison but could see that the smearing had started when this patient had been told she would never return home. With this understanding Barbara was able to challenge abuse of her patient: she called a stop to staff barricading this patient with tables in one corner of the ward because of the smearing behaviour.

Anna Dartington (1994) drew attention to the necessity of nurses having the opportunity to think about their feelings, for example to understand their anger and hatred of patients who seem to refuse to get better and thus frustrate the staff's reparative drives. If staff have the opportunity to talk about their feelings they are less likely to retaliate. Angry and provocative patients are especially vulnerable to retaliatory behaviour from carers, especially in view of the 'potential sadistic abuse of the absolute power that staff inevitably has over in-patients' (Dartington, 1994). Yet, as Dartington points out the worries about having such power are rarely talked about. The consultations with Betty and Barbara demonstrate that when there are opportunities to talk about their feelings about patients, staff can successfully challenge abusive practices on the wards.

## Pursuing suspicions of physical abuse

*As I endeavoured to pursue the suspicions of abuse, my feelings of shock, denial and anger created difficulties. It was crucial to have access to a colleague to help me process some of these feelings in order to be able to think and take action.*

Several months after offering these consultations I started working with a keyworker about a patient who was causing disturbance on the ward because he was constantly shouting day and night. He had suffered two strokes and could no longer speak, except for shouting expletives. It was also difficult to determine how much he could understand of what was said to him. I later saw this patient, whom I call Mr Mitchell, for individual therapy which is described in Chapter 4. In an early discussion with the keyworker, almost as an aside, she mentioned that she was worried about recent things which had happened to Mr Mitchell. I asked what sort of things. She told me of bruises on his shoulders and blisters on his thighs for which there was no explanation. There had been an incident when, as he was being undressed for a bath, his shoe had been taken off in such a rough manner that his toenail had been torn off. I felt stunned. I left the interview in a troubled state of mind, having arranged to meet again with the keyworker the following week. I had to go on to other meetings elsewhere. It was only in the early evening when I was about to leave the hospital that I recalled the talk with the keyworker. I felt more and more uneasy, especially because I appeared to have simply forgotten and had left the matter quite unresolved. So, before going home, I went to see my senior colleague, the clinical psychology manager. It was a great relief to talk about what I had heard from the keyworker. I felt some of my own shock and horror was understood. I then felt more able to think with my colleague about what to do. We decided that as soon as possible I would talk to the ward sister about the suspected abuse, and tell the keyworker what action I was taking.

When I met with the sister I found, on the one hand, she appeared to have some kind of explanation for each of the incidents the keyworker had raised. On the other hand, she showed some worry but implied the source of abuse, if there was any, was outside of her control. As the meeting proceeded, I began to feel that I must have imagined everything, and had it all out of proportion. Afterwards I felt alarmed again. I was unconvinced that much investigation or action would follow. I talked again with my senior colleague. We concluded that I should prepare a letter to the hospital manager and send a copy to the ward sister, outlining the substance of what I had been told and my concerns.

I was aware of worrying about the effect this action would have on my work on the ward and in the rest of the hospital. I feared I would be seen as a whistle-blower with damaging consequences for my work. I was also aware of feeling full of rage and indignation, and wanting to punish those who had committed this outrage against a helpless old man. Most of all I was shocked about how I had myself been drawn into a state of disbelief and complacency.

The keyworker's worries were subsequently investigated by the hospital management. The worries were taken very seriously. No evidence of abuse was established. The keyworker said at first she was upset that I had taken this action. Later when she discussed it with her partner he agreed with my action. She realised she felt relieved. She had only recently completed her training and was fairly new to the hospital. I think she was probably ostracised for talking to me and not long after, to my regret, she left to take up post in a different field of nursing.

*Commentary*

In a review of some of the literature on 'elder abuse' the difficulty of confronting abuse is captured in the question: 'How do I confront without sound evidence when all I have is a suspicion?' (Eastman, 1993). I think my experience of pursuing abuse shows that some of the difficulties are connected with the feelings provoked by the suspected abuse. The abuse may be so shocking and so unthinkable that there is a pressure to turn a blind eye and believe it could not happen. There is also the fear of retaliation, and the fear of being retaliatory and abusive to the suspected abusers. My experience of pursuing suspicions of abuse shows that in order to be able to think and take effective action it is important to be able to consult with an independent and neutral colleague to get help in processing these feelings.

# Summary

Individual consultations with carers can help them find meaning in older patient's behaviour which may appear meaningless, be disturbing, and provocative. Carers often have to manage very difficult feelings including hope, despair, frustration, anger, disgust and hatred. Angry older patients are particularly likely to provoke retaliatory abuse. Carers who do not have an opportunity to share and reflect upon feelings stirred from constant exposure to provocative behaviour are especially vulnerable to acting out their feelings in abusive ways. The patient's behaviour may not change but if some meaning can be found then the behaviour may be more bearable. The consultations provide an opportunity to consider the feelings stirred by the contact with an older patient, and appreciate how thinking about the feelings can help the carer better understand the patient. When the carer can feel understood and gain more understanding then there is more capacity to bear some of the older person's troublesome feelings and behaviour; and there may be closer and more rewarding contact between the carer and his or her older patient. The understanding and support provided by consultations helps carers recognise and challenge mindless and retaliatory abuse of their patients, and importantly can help prevent abuse of vulnerable older people.

# 9

# SUPPORT GROUPS FOR CARE STAFF

## Introduction

Support groups are usually created with 'the hope of getting more support from colleagues, as well as from the consultant (who conducts the group), so as to cope better with painful aspects of the work' (Bolton and Zagier Roberts, 1994, p. 156). Working psychodynamically with support groups means silently monitoring, but not interpreting, the transference and counter-transference with the aim 'to promote an atmosphere of containment of anxiety rather than evacuation and enactment' (Hess, 2001, p. 122). Hess makes the important point that support groups may be the only occasion in the week when staff feel that their difficulties in the work can be acknowledged and thought about. Support groups are not intended to be group therapy, but support groups may be therapeutic. The therapeutic benefit of such groups can come from 'conveying to a staff team the willingness to "stay with" their particular work difficulties over a long time' (Hess, 2001, p. 128).

It is important to help staff to understand more about their roles and the organisational resources and limitations which may facilitate or hinder staff fulfilling their roles. Support groups are particularly important in helping staff manage the turmoil and upheaval of organisational change (Morante, 2005). Bolton and Zagier Roberts warn of the need to be alert to covert and unconscious aims of the group which may throw the group off course, and of being drawn into a process in which the support group is 'making bearable what should not be borne' (p. 165). Another useful warning is that there is often an underlying pressure to establish support groups as a way of locating institutional problems in the groups, encouraging a view that such problems are a result of personal failure on the part of staff (Dartington, 1993). Accordingly due weight needs to be given to organisational constraints, such as under-staffing and cuts in services, which staff support groups are usually impotent to influence.

An account of consultancy to a support group for members of a psychiatric team working with older people described how the emotional world of patients can get into the staff who work with them. The authors concluded that 'themes of fragility of boundaries, of fragmentation of the self, loss of identity, of failing potency and powers, loss of energy and function, each of which can be part and parcel of the elderly patient's experience, get inside the inner worlds of staff along with an accompanying undercurrent of persecutory guilt' (Dennis and Armstrong, 2007, p. 158).

In the work I shall report the *aims* of the staff support groups were to:

- help the staff in their care role by offering a time and place in which there can be some reflection on their emotional experience of caring for older people who are physically or mentally frail
- encourage staff to think about their patients' feelings about being in long stay care, showing the staff that some of their own feelings may be unconscious communications from their patients
- understand staff feelings about developments and changes within the organisation, and discuss how these feelings may affect their work
- think about but not interpret the transference and counter-transference dynamics in the support group, and
- think about the relationship between the staff support group and the organisation as a whole.

It is crucial that support groups have the backing of the management and leaders of the organisation (Robertson and Davison, 1997). I was fortunate because the senior management in the hospital, with whom I consulted regularly, valued and encouraged the support groups in the hospital. I shall describe staff support group meetings for staff on a long stay, (or 'continuing care') ward for very frail older people. A description of the kinds of illnesses from which these patients suffered is given in Chapter 6. The meetings were held on the wards because for reasons of cost it was not possible to provide staff to cover wards during a support group. We met each week in the staff office which overlooked the wards, sometimes without one or two staff who were on duty on the ward, and often with interruptions from the phone and personal callers to the ward. There were usually four to six staff present at each meeting, a mix of qualified and unqualified nursing staff, mostly all female staff because there were few male staff. As a result of the shift system, usually only one or two of those present would have attended the previous meeting. Only day staff attended the support groups. There were also 'agency' or 'bank' staff on all the wards to cover temporary absences, and sometimes they attended the support groups.

The support group I shall describe on the 'York' ward had met for over a year when I had to discontinue the meetings because of other commitments. A few months later, as a result of some changes in my schedule and a request to continue the group from the staff on the York ward, I resumed the group. I shall give an account of meetings over a period of six months after the group resumed. Barbara and Melody, with whom I described consultations in relation to keyworking in the previous chapter, were staff on the York ward and attended some of the meetings. During the six months in which these meetings were held, amidst crises and changes that beset an organisation like the NHS, there were major upheavals for the staff: in an effort to make necessary savings the health authority encouraged staff to apply for redundancy and early retirement; after several years' delay, plans to construct new buildings for the long stay service were given the go-ahead; the management of the service was put out to tender for bids from the private sector; and the health authority was to merge with another authority to form a 'Trust'.

## The York Support Group

### Worries about change bringing staff too close to their patients

*Changes in the service led the staff to experience feelings of loss and rejection and thus feel more and more identified with their older patients.*

At the first meeting after resuming the support group Gloria, the ward sister, was angry with the other staff. She complained they had little to say even though they had said they wanted the group. She was angry too about the hospital manager criticising the ward saying it should be more homely like the other wards in the hospital. Gloria argued that individual homes are different so why shouldn't the wards be different? She felt particularly rebuked because the manager said there was a lot of tension between staff on the ward. When I said she seemed to feel that the tension was her fault she visibly softened in her demeanour and other staff started contributing. A young auxiliary, Fay, said she thought the tension was connected with the uncertainty about the future of the hospital, especially since the senior staff were leaving. (The care group manager and the senior nursing advisor, Diana, had both left within the previous two months.) Gloria agreed with Fay and with sadness she said that she couldn't go to Diana for support anymore.

In a meeting the following month Gloria looked glum and sat with her back to the other staff, staring out onto the ward. Melody spoke of the plans for the new buildings and the land on which they were to be built. She was worried that the buildings could not accommodate all the patients because they would be too small and there was too little land to build larger units. Other staff joined in correcting this perception, though they added their own misgivings. There was concern about how the patients would be allocated to the different sites. It was thought they would probably go to the site nearest to where their relatives lived, which would mean they would be dispersed. I said I thought the staff were also worried that the patients would die rather than move. They agreed saying that they could tell who would die in the move. Two of the older nursing staff, Barbara and Liz, said that they felt the trained staff would no longer be wanted in the new buildings. They recalled other moves during the years in the hospital, sometimes at very short notice and with little preparation. For example Barbara described a whole ward being moved after having been told only a few days before.

A month later the staff received a circular encouraging them to apply for redundancy or early retirement. There was an atmosphere of excitement as Barbara and Liz anticipated taking early retirement. With a laugh I commented that it was like a leaving party! After a while the staff became subdued. One of the senior staff quoted a younger colleague from another ward who had said that the older staff should go to make way for the younger ones. The older staff present were very angry. I said I thought the younger staff were doubtless worried about their future. Katie, a young auxiliary, agreed saying she had a large debt she was paying off and was fearful about what she would do if she was out of a job. Rose, an older auxiliary, looked upset and told us her husband was now out of work and they had a mortgage to pay.

There was also some talk about news that management of the service was to be put out to tender to the private sector. The staff were worried because the private sector mainly managed 'part III accommodation' (suitable for less dependent and more mobile patients) and had little knowledge of the type of care needed for the highly dependent patients in this long stay hospital. Someone then mentioned that the ceiling on one of the other wards was said to be 'caving in'. I said that the service would cave in without them. They looked touched and sad. I asked why couldn't *they* organise a bid for the tender, after all, they knew about this service.

## Commentary

The first meeting shows how feelings of criticism and failure can be passed down the institutional hierarchy. Staff in a service for older people are particularly susceptible to feelings of failure because of their helplessness to improve their patients' physical state or prevent them from dying. Moreover, the service as a whole was in great difficulty. The health authority was in a financial crisis and decisions had already been taken to make cuts in services which would have hard consequences. However, as Tim Dartington (1993) has pointed out, there is a danger that a support group can collude to maintain a view of the hospital as a caring system, in which such difficulties are only understood as personal failures.

In particular, the material shows how the ward sister, Gloria, who was consumed with feeling criticised, passed those feelings onto the junior staff when she attacked them for not speaking. In turn she had probably been the recipient of similar feelings from the hospital manager, who had lost her two senior colleagues. I think these departures felt rejecting and were destabilising. The care group manager, who left, had been openly critical of his own manager. Pointing out that Gloria felt personally responsible, challenged this belief. She then seemed to feel less angry, and allowed some space for the junior staff to talk about their feelings, particularly sad feelings about the events in the hospital.

The next meeting shows how a move to two new smaller buildings seemed to provoke infantile feelings of being small and abandoned, expressed in the anxieties about the buildings being too small to accommodate all the patients. It was important to draw out the staff's worries about patients dying. It is well-known that during such moves there is a high mortality rate of older patients (Davenhill, 2007b, p. 205). The staff often found it difficult to talk about their feelings about patients dying, perhaps because the staff were so frequently exposed to death. I think at this time it was more difficult for the staff to talk about losing their patients because they were confronted with so many other losses. The staff felt unwanted by the health authority which threatened to abandon the service to the private sector. The older trained staff, often quite identified with their patients, anticipated they would be rejected in favour of untrained, younger carers. The move also revived memories of other losses.

The later material shows how the staff tried to manage the burden of these painful feelings. The excitement about the possible early retirement and redundancy payments indicated an almost manic denial of feelings of rejection which soon gave way to a more persecutory split between the older and younger staff, in a rejection of the old by the young. The group thus became consumed with feelings very closely resembling those of their older patients. It reminds me of the practice in some cultures where the old who were ailing were ejected from their communities and left to die (de Beauvoir, 1970), of course not so different from the practice of admitting these older patients into a long stay hospital. The split between young and old staff seemed like an attempt by the younger staff to rid themselves of these feelings. By my attending to some of the younger staff's fears, there was a reduction in the splitting, a 'caving in' of some of the persecutory defences against the worries and some space for sad and angry feelings. I felt it was important to acknowledge the contribution of the staff because of their sense of being unvalued. Also I thought it useful to challenge their sense of helplessness about making a bid for the tender.

## Containment helping staff regain their roles and achievements

*Note the development in the meetings when the staff felt some of their anxieties about the changes in the hospital were being thought about and understood. The staff were then able to bring up concerns about their patients and acknowledge satisfaction gained from the work.*

When I met the staff after the holiday the meeting was unusually late in starting. I had come back with a haircut and there were jokes about my 'short hair'. Gloria was particularly angry. She kept joining and then leaving the meeting which made me angry. There seemed to be confusion and fear about the tender. The internal management was now putting in a bid. The staff complained about a new senior nurse, Marilyn, who was not present. She was described as throwing her weight around and treating the others as if they didn't know anything. I talked about the difficulty of the feelings about not knowing what was going to happen to the service and the problem of what to do with these feelings.

A month later the staff were in low spirits. It seemed staff in the long stay service would not after all be eligible for redundancy or early retirement because of the changes in the long stay service. They talked of recent thefts of some patients' money from the ward. There was suspicion that a member of staff was responsible and there was a tense atmosphere in the meeting. I said I felt they were very unhappy about what might be stolen from them, like their jobs, and now it seemed they would not even be entitled to redundancy or early retirement. Some of the staff sadly agreed, one saying there was 'nothing left' and that it was hard to continue working with all the uncertainty.

The next fortnight there was a moving discussion about difficult feelings whenever patients died. Two young auxiliaries talked of how a recent death on the ward reminded them of friends who had died. Rose, an older auxiliary, spoke of how very upset she had been about the death of one of her patients for whom she was keyworker. The new staff nurse, Marilyn, was present and seemed quite withdrawn. When I asked her what she thought about what had been said, she told us she was a born-again Christian and had no fears or upsets about death.

A fortnight later the thieving was brought up again. I repeated my interpretation about what the staff feared would be stolen from them in terms of redundancy payment or job security. Some money had been found on the ward and there was some confusion about whether it belonged to the patients or staff. I talked of the confusion resulting from the staff feeling so much like the patients when the staff faced so much loss themselves because of the move and possible change of management.

The next fortnight there was a lighter but more thoughtful atmosphere in the meeting. A young auxiliary, Vera, talked about one of her patients, George, for whom she was keyworker. Vera felt she could not work with George and that he would be better off with someone else as keyworker. He was slightly mobile and kept falling. Recently he had a bad fall. Vera took him to the casualty department for an X-ray. Apparently he kept calling her his wife and embarrassed her by making sexual overtures. I asked the staff to tell me what they knew about George. They all joined in with different bits of information.

George was suffering from Parkinson's Disease and dementia. He had been on the ward for just a few months. His wife had breast cancer. His daughter had recently separated from her husband and she suffered from problems with alcohol. Some of the staff knew George's son, a handsome man who had been to the local grammar school. When the son turned up on the ward they thought he was an airline pilot in his uniform and then realised that he was 'merely a bus driver'.

I talked about the tragedies in George's life, his illnesses, his wife's cancer and perhaps his fear that she might die, as well as the likely ambitions and disappointments he felt about his children. He suffered the pain that his wife had become a visitor in his life. In his confused state Vera probably seemed more like a wife to him since she spent so much time with him and looked after him in such an intimate way like a wife would do. I said he probably felt quite frightened in casualty, perhaps he feared he was dying.

Some of the staff complained that George had been kept waiting for five hours at casualty. If he had been seen more quickly it would have been less disturbing for him and everyone else. I reminded them of the chaos at the general hospital which was likely to merge with another hospital into a new 'Trust'; and the chaos in this hospital and how difficult it was to think under such conditions. They then talked about the uncertain future. The older staff still were hoping for early retirement, whereas the younger staff were feeling optimistic. Vera said she planned to take up nurse training and Katie said she hoped for a new job as a carer when the hospital moved. Again Marilyn looked withdrawn. When I encouraged her to speak she said how much better the staff morale was here than in another hospital where she also worked part-time. She described this other hospital as a neglected work environment with a hostile and suspicious staff. She wondered if the better morale here was connected with these support meetings.

At the next meeting, George was discussed again. He was being taken to the general hospital to visit his wife who had been suddenly admitted, dying from cancer. A lot of concern was expressed about him. Vera said she was getting on better with him and had not pursued her request to change from being his keyworker. There was a delay in taking him to the general hospital because it was discovered he was wearing someone else's trousers. He was upset and his own trousers had gone missing. The two senior staff, Barbara and Liz, took the matter in hand, found the trousers and completed the arrangements for George to see his wife. They returned to the meeting expressing their pleasure about having sorted it out.

A fortnight later we had a final meeting before my summer holiday. Barbara and Liz had been to see the hospital manager about their future. Even though the personnel department had given them details of their likely redundancy payments, they were told they would not be able to take redundancy or early retirement because staff could not be released from the long stay service. Union meetings had also been held about the possible consequences if staff were transferred to a private company. It seemed there could be no long term guarantee that conditions of service or pensions would be protected. The staff were very angry. I said their hopes had been raised only to be dashed.

There was a lot of worry about the tender for the hospital which would not be decided for another two months. It was feared the tender would be awarded to a private company. The staff exchanged worrying stories of their own and others' experiences of working for private nursing homes. In one home where a former auxiliary was now working, for less money, the patients were all taken out of bed at an early hour, kept waiting in their bedclothes and given a poor breakfast. Food and provisions for patients and staff were severely rationed there because of costs. The talk became more and more rapid, interspersed with tense laughter. They struggled with feelings of anxiety and despair. I said I thought they felt unwanted and unappreciated by the health authority which they felt intended to abandon them to a private company.

## Commentary

The Easter holiday break galvanised feelings about loss in the group. In their transference to me the staff felt abandoned over the holiday. These feelings can be seen in the way the staff kept me waiting to start, as I had kept them waiting over the holiday and cut them short of support, like, as they remarked, my hair had been cut short. In my counter-transference about Gloria, who kept coming and going, I experienced something of the staff anger with my coming and going. I did not interpret these transferential feelings because this would have encouraged a therapeutic dependency on me which would be inappropriate to a support group. Instead I saw my task as being to think about what light these counter-transference feelings could shed on how staff felt in their roles in the hospital.

The staff were especially vulnerable to angry feelings because of their grief about losses they anticipated in connection with changes in the hospital. My interpretation about their anger with Marilyn addressed some of the anger with management for leaving the staff in a great deal of uncertainty about the future. It was my hope too that this interpretation would ease their relationship with Marilyn from some of the feelings which seemed displaced onto her. It was especially important to help staff be more aware of their anger to avoid these feelings being expressed against the patients.

It was important that the discussion about the thefts which was marked by suspicion and insinuation did not turn into a witch hunt for the culprit. It was not the task of the support group to pursue the guilty party. The usefulness of interpreting the thefts in the context of developments in the hospital was that staff were thereby enabled to express more of their grief about the future. This work paved the way for the staff's feelings of grief about recent deaths on the ward. The material shows how staff not only experience the pain of losing their patients but have memories revived about their loved ones who have died. However, I think Marilyn's born-again Christian position probably indicated some split off manic defence in the group against these sad, depressive feelings.

The further discussion of the thefts allowed the theme of loss for the staff to be further worked through and revealed another strand of meaning for the staff: how the losses and feelings of rejection they faced brought them much closer to their patients' grief with some resulting confusion between themselves and their patients. After I articulated this source of confusion with the patients, there were signs of relief and significantly, at the next meeting, there was the first substantial discussion about a patient since the group had resumed. Thus, working through some of the grief about the organisational changes and some of the ensuing role confusion enabled the staff to get back into role and to think with concern about their patients. They were helped to reinstate a useful split allowing them to differentiate themselves from their patients.

It is interesting that George, the patient the staff brought for discussion, encapsulated some of their own worries. He suffered many painful losses and disappointments in his illnesses and faced the death of his wife. He then suffered a fall and was kept waiting a long time to know if anything had been broken. The staff too were struggling to face the losses in the move to new buildings which would probably sever some of the staff and patient relationships. Like George they suffered a fall in their expectations about redundancy and early retirement payments; they were kept waiting because it was still unknown who would be allocated to which site and if there would be new private management which might mean further losses. The way George's problems reflected their own probably contributed to the feeling of him being unmanageable which was voiced by his keyworker. The opportunity to discuss their feelings about George helped the staff disentangle themselves from George and enjoy a sense of satisfaction in their work with him. In the discussion about George the staff were working consciously on George's problems and at an unconscious level they were working on their issues of loss. In the context of a support group it would have been inappropriate to make such an interpretative link which could have implied that I thought they were only working on their own issues and that I disregarded their genuine concern for George.

The final meeting before the holiday in which the staff were again consumed with anger and worry about the future, shows the difficulty they had in sustaining thoughtfulness about the patients when the support of the groups was about to be interrupted and when they were assailed by fears about changes in the hospital. They were being abandoned by their health authority management and by me who was going on holiday.

# Summary

Support groups are important for helping staff manage the feelings stirred by working with older, physically and mentally frail people. Carers for these older people are vulnerable to projected feelings of rejection, helplessness and loss; and all the more so when, as in the group described, organisational changes mean staff face much uncertainty and insecurity about their future, especially in a society in which ageism is prevalent, as I have discussed in Chapter 7. The support groups provide time and space for staff to reflect upon and express their feelings about the work and the organisation. Staff can be helped to see how their own feelings may be similar in some respects to how their patients feel, but also to differentiate themselves from their patients and to hold onto a sense of their skills and competency.

It is crucial that staff have opportunities to express their anger and frustration about their work which is sometimes inevitable in caring for very ill older people, and about organisational constraints and changes they may have little power to influence. In the absence of opportunities to express such feelings there is the danger that anger and frustration may be acted out against the patients. There is also the need for staff to grieve, to share sadness and sorrow as they face, again and again, the deaths of their patients, which bring reminders of other painful losses as well as of their own mortality. A space for grieving demonstrates recognition and support for the staff's love and concern for their patients, and the reparative wishes, interests, skills and sensitivities which they bring to this work.

# 10

## TEACHING AND LEARNING ABOUT THERAPY WITH OLDER PEOPLE

### Introduction

In contemporary psychodynamic counselling and psychotherapy the use of the counsellor's or therapist's own feelings are central to the work. The centrality of one's own feelings, the counter-transference, is a significant development in psychoanalytic theory and practice. In the beginning of psychoanalysis Freud saw counter-transference essentially as an obstacle to the therapeutic work. In particular he believed that if the therapist's transferences to the client were not adequately analysed they could impede the therapeutic work. It was for this reason Freud and other early analysts came to emphasise the importance of personal psychotherapy as an essential part of therapeutic training. However, by the middle of the last century, thinking about counter-transference changed. On the one hand counter-transference was opened up as a concept to include all the therapist's feelings in the therapeutic encounter and, on the other hand counter-transference was seen a central means of understanding unconscious communication between client and therapist. Paula Heimann (1950), who led these developments, indicated that the point of personal psychotherapy was not to analyse away the trainee therapist's feelings but rather to enable him or her to 'sustain' the feelings instead of discharging them in some sort of action. Later developments have furthered the understanding of the therapeutic process as one in which the therapist is receptive to and offers 'containment' for the client's feelings, especially those feelings which the client may find unbearable (Bion, 1962).

A further important development has been the introduction of observation of mother and infant as a part of psychodynamic and psychoanalytic training. Esther Bick (1968) pioneered observational studies for child psychotherapists at the Tavistock Clinic in London, whereby a trainee therapist visits a mother and baby for one hour once a week for the first two years of the baby's life. The trainee takes up the role as an observer, he or she does not initiate any interaction but only actively engages with mother and infant when invited to do so. The trainee takes no notes but following the observation writes a 'process recording' of everything he or she can recall of the observation: a moment-by-moment description of what was seen and heard and very importantly an account of the observer's feelings during the observation. These recordings are then discussed with other trainees in a weekly seminar led by a senior therapist (Rustin, 1989).

Savi McKenzie-Smith (1992) introduced the use of this observational technique for understanding more about the emotional experience of older people. Subsequently, some courses offering training in therapeutic work with older people have included observational studies as a key element in the training (Davenhill, Balfour and Rustin, 2007). I encourage clinical psychology trainees who are on placement with me to take up an observational study in settings such as community day centres, continuing care wards or dementia units. The observation provides an experience that allows the trainee an opportunity to be with older people without the pressure of having to make a therapeutic intervention, but with time to reflect on the older person's experience in the light of the trainee's own emotional reactions.

When trainees start therapeutic work they bring to supervision process recordings of the interaction between the client and themselves in particular sessions. They are again encouraged to reflect on their own emotional reactions during the sessions. I do not usually sit in or arrange for trainees to make a recording of their sessions. The reason for this is that the focus of the supervision is the client in the mind of the trainee. The supervision models a containing process in which as supervisor I aim to be receptive to the trainees' feelings, helping them to manage their worries, and reflect on their feelings as a way of further understanding the client. It is important to think about the impact that the client has on the trainee and the impact that the trainee has on the client. Like all of us, trainees have their own vulnerabilities, and it is particularly these vulnerabilities to which clients are acutely attuned in the unconscious communication of their own worries and vulnerabilities.

There are of course many other issues which need to be addressed in supervision, especially in matters of therapeutic technique, framing and timing of interpretations to bring the unconscious into conscious awareness, diagnosis and psychodynamic formulation, therapeutic boundaries, ethics and confidentiality, difference and diversity and so on. In this chapter I will touch on some of these other issues but the focus will be on how to make therapeutic use of the counter-transference.

## Disability and vulnerability

*A trainee's disability was a means by which a patient could make a link with the trainee and convey feelings about vulnerability when words were failing because of dementia. As the trainee felt easier about acknowledging his disability he could then think creatively about how it might be used for purposes of unconscious communication by his clients.*

I would like to describe some work with Dominik Ritter, who undertook an observation of an older man in a dementia unit. Mr Stringer was in his seventies. He was referred to the unit because his wife could no longer manage to look after him at home. Ten years previously he had started developing dementia. Dominik became interested because the nursing staff in the unit had much difficulty communicating with Mr Stringer and were particularly unsure about what this man could understand. Mr Stringer usually only spoke with isolated words. Sometimes he seemed to understand and then sometimes not. Dominik thought he might try to assess Mr Stringer's comprehension by showing him cards with words or pictures and by trying writing or drawing as an alternative means of communication. At first Dominik was enthusiastic about Mr Stringer's responses to the cards and thought it would be possible to establish what vocabulary Mr Stringer had left. Dominik was inclined to ask Mr Stringer many questions to which Mr Stringer sometimes responded but often ignored. Sometimes he became quite agitated. I suggested to Dominik that if Mr Stringer was losing his capacities then it could feel very frustrating to be questioned and either not being able to understand the question or to articulate a reply. Dominik soon gave up this approach and took up an observer role, simply sitting alongside Mr Stringer, trying to think about his own feelings when with Mr Stringer and what it might be like for Mr Stringer.

Gradually Mr Stringer seemed to be more at ease with Dominik and pleased when Dominik came to see him. On one occasion when Dominik sat with Mr Stringer he saw that Mr Stringer was taking a lively interest in what the nursing staff were doing and said 'nice'. He touched Dominik's arm and said 'my friend'. Later he suddenly reached out towards Dominik's eyes. Dominik drew back, startled and frightened that Mr Stringer might injure him.

When we discussed this observation in supervision, I suggested to Dominik that perhaps in reaching out to Dominik's eyes Mr Stringer wanted Dominik to know something of Mr Stringer's own sense of fear and vulnerability. The next week Dominik brought a further observation. When Dominik arrived he noticed that Mr Stringer looked especially dishevelled. However he smiled when Dominik sat with him. He was burping a lot and stroking his cheek and hands. He looked down and made no eye contact with Dominik. Then he reached out for one of Dominik's boots. He touched the boot and then lifted it up.

In supervision Dominik had various thoughts about the touching of the boot. He wondered if Mr Stringer had found a safer form of contact than the previous week when he had reached out for Dominik's eyes; or he speculated whether touching the boot had anything to do with what he knew about Mr Stringer's history and interest in ballroom dancing.

As I heard this observation and Dominik's thoughts, I recalled my first meeting with Dominik. I had noticed his boots and thought what an unusual style which I attributed to his youthful tastes. It was only later that I could manage to take in that these were special shoes because of a disability which was also evident in Dominik's gait, again something I had failed to register earlier. I think my difficulty in thinking about Dominik's disability reflects something of the pain of acknowledging handicap either in oneself or others. Valerie Sinason (1992), who has written eloquently about mental handicap, reminds us that we all struggle not to handicap ourselves and suffer the pain of recognising the discrepancy between how we are and what we might have been or what we once were. But for some the damage to their body or brain means this discrepancy is very great and brings much pain.

As gently as I could I talked to Dominik about the meaning of his boots as they signalled his disability, and how this might help us understand more of Mr Stringer's communication to him. Dominik was able to acknowledge his difficulty in admitting these signs of disability. He soon saw that Mr Stringer may have wanted to make a link with him through the boot: as if to say 'here's someone who knows about disability, perhaps he can understand how disabled and vulnerable I feel'.

Sometime later Dominik started working with an 87 year-old woman, Mrs Carlisle, who had been admitted in a very withdrawn and depressed state. She was practically mute and had to be actively encouraged to eat and drink. Dominik began by going to sit alongside Mrs Carlisle where she sat in the unit. She usually ignored him as she did other staff and patients. Dominik again reflected on his own feelings when with her and tried to think how she might feel. Occasionally as a result of these reflections he would offer some thoughts about Mrs Carlisle's feelings, not as questions but simply as statements which she could consider or ignore.

During one observation Mrs Carlisle started hitting her forehead, firstly with the back of one hand and then with the other. It reminded Dominik of an experience he had with an autistic teenager who used to bang his head and scratch his face; he also thought of a video he'd seen of a brain injured man with whom staff were trying to work and who became enraged, biting his shirt. So Dominik spoke about how angry Mrs Carlisle might feel, even angry with Dominik and perhaps wanting to hit him. Mrs Carlisle did not respond but Dominik noticed, in contrast to previous occasions, this time she was leaning towards him and she had opened her eyes which were usually firmly shut. She repeated the hitting of her forehead and again Dominik spoke of her anger. Mrs Carlisle then took out both her hearing aids. Dominik appreciated she was making her anger with him very clear: she didn't want to hear anything more he had to say. Sometime later Dominik noticed that Mrs Carlisle was calmer. She seemed to be playing with her hearing aids by using one hearing aid to pick up the other. Dominik wondered to himself whether she was referring to his disability and commenting on one disabled person trying to support another.

Gradually Mrs Carlisle's depression lifted. She began interacting on the ward. Two weeks after the previous observation when Dominik visited her in her room, Mrs Carlisle said she thought Dominik would like to see her. Dominik asked her if that was agreeable to her. She said yes and accompanied him to his consulting room. Dominik continued to see Mrs Carlisle for weekly supportive therapy sessions until the end of his placement some weeks later.

I thought Dominik was developing a fine sensitivity in his capacity to observe and reflect on his thoughts and feelings. I was impressed too by his ability to draw on his associations to the behaviour of the patient. He had also become more at ease with thinking about his disability, and could playfully imagine how it might be being used for purposes of unconscious communication. I think these developments helped him connect with Mrs Carlisle whilst she was otherwise withdrawn and inaccessible. When she had made some recovery this connection doubtless facilitated an alliance for therapeutic work.

Mrs King, another of Dominik's clients, made an explicit reference to his disability. It was during her final session with Dominik before he left the placement. Mrs King opened the session by asking Dominik if he went swimming. Dominik was a bit thrown by the question. He replied 'not recently'. Mrs King went on to recommend that Dominik should swim because it would help straighten out his legs. Dominik felt embarrassed and rather hurt to have attention drawn to his disability in this way. Later Mrs King complained about the doctors. She said she no longer trusted them. She was thinking of getting legal aid. She also spoke critically of the nurses not doing their jobs properly and not even making her bed adequately. She then talked about her plans to buy a caravan and live on a camping site. Towards the end of the session Mrs King asked to leave early. She said how much she had enjoyed their 'chats'. Dominik was left feeling rather sad.

Mrs King had a long psychiatric history. She had spent a considerable time on an adult psychiatric ward before being transferred to the older people's unit and had not lived in her own flat for a long time. It was unlikely she would able to live independently again. She had made a good contact with Dominik. I said to him that I thought she felt terribly hurt and betrayed by his departure which was another loss. But her hurt, vulnerability and sadness were lodged in Dominik, whereas she was quite contemptuous of Dominik like the doctors and nurses. I think she could only manage the leaving in this 'sour grapes' way, as though there was no one to miss. She might as well leave first and leave early. Unlike Dominik, who could move on, she now faced being in an institution for the rest of her life.

## Discharging feelings through questions

*Questions can be used to expel painful feelings back into the client.*

Sometimes questions which ostensibly are a way of seeking information discharge uncomfortable feelings and knowledge. In the first weeks of a placement trainees tend to bring sessions to supervision which are full of questions to their clients, which I think reflect more about the trainees' worries than the need for information. For example Dominik reported some work with Mrs Goring who had been referred because of concerns about changes in her behaviour and problems with her memory. Before her retirement she held a senior academic post, but since then she sometimes had difficulty in expressing herself and had become quite forgetful. Some emotional factors were thought to be contributing to her difficulties but there was concern about possible organic causes.

Mrs Goring began her first meeting with Dominik by declaring, with much irritation, that there was nothing the matter with her, she didn't know why she was seeing him, and after all she'd got full marks when tested by the consultant in the memory clinic. The interview proceeded in this prickly way. Dominik was aware of feeling more and more anxious. After some unsuccessful attempts to engage Mrs Goring, he asked her to tell him how she was feeling by giving a rating out of ten on a 'comfort – distress' scale. She answered 'five'. Dominik then asked her what she did in her spare time. She gave a cryptic reply. I said to Dominik that I thought he already knew the answer to his question about her comfort through his own increasing discomfort. It seemed difficult to think about a discomfort that probably was connected with this woman's dread that she was suffering from dementia, a diagnosis that was later confirmed by a psychoneurological assessment. What seemed to have been lodged very powerfully in Dominik was a terror that felt unthinkable. His question to her was an unconscious way of trying to put this terror back into the client.

Another trainee gradually discovered the value of resisting what he described as 'probing'. Instead he tried to understand what might be preventing his client from telling him about herself. He had been seeing an older woman suffering from depression for once weekly therapy for some months. She seemed to be stuck in grief for her husband who died several years ago. She said little about her life and gave a rather idealised picture of her marriage. The trainee came to appreciate that his client was particularly worried about how he might react to anything she said. On one occasion she mentioned that she was concerned about making her house more comfortable. The trainee interpreted that he thought she was also concerned about making him comfortable. She did not reply but later in the session for the first time she admitted some severe difficulties in the relationship with her husband.

## Guilt and vulnerability

*Feelings of ambivalence and guilt stirred in the trainee came to be understood as an early communication that belied the client's words.*

Some weeks after starting her training placement, a trainee Michele Cloherty was asked by one of our Community Psychiatric Nurses to see Mrs Holly. The CPN thought Mrs Holly could benefit from some therapy to help her with some tragic bereavements, all of which had occurred within a few months. Firstly, her husband whom she had been nursing had died; later one of her daughters and then a son died. Michele was asked to see Mrs Holly in her home because Mrs Holly, then in her seventies, had physical problems which prevented her leaving the house. When Michele met Mrs Holly, she told Michele she was particularly close to the daughter who died. She said she was unable to cry about these deaths. She described how her father had died when she was just seven years old. She was the eldest and felt she had to be the responsible one. She later said to Michele she felt she had to be 'mother and father' to her mother and siblings. She felt she must not cry.

During the assessment meeting Mrs Holly revealed a strict and punitive Catholic upbringing and relentless tragedies throughout her life. She was brought up to believe in a fiery hell. She said to Michele that she now felt numb, miserable and burning in hell. Many years previously she had suffered from alcoholism. She had therapy for six years which she found very helpful. Mrs Holly said she felt ready for therapy again. Whilst presenting this material to me Michele became upset. She confided that she felt very guilty because, although she felt extreme sorrow for Mrs Holly, she simply felt she could not bear to take her on for therapy. Michele was by now well-established in the placement. She had started regular work with several clients. She had shown much courage in engaging with clients who presented difficult and painful problems. Michele had also been assiduous in arranging to start personal psychotherapy to support her learning in the placement. So I was somewhat surprised to hear her reservations about offering therapy to this client, though I was glad that she was able to be open about her feelings. I assured her that there was no compulsion to see the client for therapy. I also talked about how we all have our vulnerabilities and limits about what we can manage; and how important it is to acknowledge these limits, and not to try to be omnipotent. However, I thought it important to try to understand more about this reaction. I suggested Michele extend the assessment period a little, without any presumption that she would continue seeing the client. I said 'just see how it goes'. Michele was visibly relieved. She agreed to see Mrs Holly for a couple more assessment meetings.

When Michele presented Mrs Holly again in supervision she said she felt much easier when she returned to Mrs Holly. She decided she could after all continue to see Mrs Holly. We discussed this further and agreed that when Michele next saw Mrs Holly, she would arrange to visit her for weekly sessions until the end of the placement. Mrs Holly seemed pleased but when Michele arrived the next week Mrs Holly was unprepared for her. She said she had forgotten about Michele's visit. Thereafter various problems occurred around the boundaries: several times there were friends or relatives present when Michele arrived. We decided that Michele would be firm about the boundaries. When others were present she would not stay but simply say that she would return at the same time next week. On one occasion Michele arrived to find Mrs Holly going to hospital in an ambulance following an asthma attack. The next week she wondered with Michele how much such attacks were 'in the mind'.

I talked with Michele about how difficult it can be for clients, who are seen at home or in an institution, not to attend the sessions, though clearly Mrs Holly had found ways. It is important to respect these defences and to try to understand them. Michele reported a session in which Mrs Holly again talked about the death of her favourite daughter but added she felt unable to cry. She said she felt physically sick and pointed to her abdomen. As I heard this session I was reminded of Michele's initial reluctance when she felt she could not bear to see Mrs Holly for therapy. I said to Michele that, despite Mrs Holly's apparent eagerness to have therapy, now we could see how Michele's early feelings spoke of a profound and understandable reluctance within Mrs Holly about venturing into thinking about a lifetime of dreadful loss and pain.

## Terror and dependency

*A client's terrors of dependency were very soon conveyed through the trainee's feelings.*

Another trainee, Gary Walker, had a curious sensation when accompanying Mrs Rice to the consulting room for a first meeting. Mrs Rice was in her seventies and though physically fit she followed Gary to the room very slowly. He told me he felt as if he was 'dragging a lamb to the slaughter'. Mrs Rice had a history of depression and some previous failed attempts to help her. She was admitted to the in-patient unit following a suicide attempt. Once in the consulting room Mrs Rice was eager to talk to Gary, so much so that she spoke continuously until the end of the interview. Gary felt there was almost no need or opportunity to say anything. On the next occasion Gary saw Mrs Rice she came more quickly to the consulting room, and again talked practically non-stop. In these meetings she described some recent events that were particularly distressing to her and were perhaps triggers for her depression.

In my discussions with Gary about these interviews what was conspicuous was that although Mrs Rice spoke of her early life, particularly warmly about her father, she made no reference to her mother. It was only towards the end of the second interview that Mrs Rice said very stridently she did not want to be like her mother who was a burden and expected Mrs Rice to care for her.

Mrs Rice became adamant she did not want to stay in the in-patient unit or engage in any of the occupational therapy activities there. When she was discharged a few weeks later, she said she found the meetings with Gary helpful. She wanted to continue seeing him as an out-patient. However, she did not return to see Gary despite his efforts to encourage her to do so. Gary had enjoyed seeing Mrs Rice and felt hopeful about working with her. He was left feeling disappointed.

It is clear that Mrs Rice found it very difficult to depend on others to care for her. Brian Martindale's (1989a) work has revealed the link between early experiences of failed dependency which then lead to a dread of dependency in later life. Mrs Rice's story about her mother being such a burden may be what Freud described as a 'screen memory' and refer to earlier experiences when Mrs Rice felt burdened by a mother who could not hold her in her mind and perhaps exposed her to terrors of being unheld, terrors of falling to pieces. I think when Gary had the sensation of 'dragging a lamb to the slaughter' he may have picked up through his own feelings how Mrs Rice's vulnerable self felt terrified of being let down again. To put this another way, her infantile dread was that if she allowed herself to be held she would again be dropped and exposed to terrors of annihilation. In the first meetings with Mrs Rice she talked non-stop as though she had no need of hearing anything from Gary and indeed he felt there was no need for him to say anything. Mrs Rice's continuous talking may be how she tried to hold herself together with the sound of her own voice, rather than depend on Gary. When she later raised Gary's hopes about engaging in some therapeutic work and then dashed them by abruptly discontinuing the sessions, she may also have been conveying some of her own early disappointment.

## Commentary

The discoveries that led to appreciating the contribution counter-transference makes to understanding the unconscious communication between therapist and client occurred in parallel with Klein's develop-ment of Freud's concept of projection. Paula Heimann's work (1950) heralds the changes in thinking about counter-transference. She was at the time a close colleague of Klein and Heimann's thinking about counter-transference draws on understanding about projective identi-fication. Thus feelings and states of mind which are felt to be unbearable are understood to be projected into the therapist for containment. At worst these are hardly states of mind at all but represent psychotic aspects of the mind that work against the mind itself, and can 'invade and deaden the mind' (Caper, 1999, p. 148), and present enormous challenges for containment.

Projective identification involves a delusion which denies separateness. The one who projects is effectively treating the other person as an extension of him- or herself. When the person who receives the projection identifies with the feelings it becomes a shared delusion as though there is a merging with the other. Projective identification is therefore the basis of a powerful form of empathy with unconscious feelings and, for patients suffering from dementia, with feelings for which there are no longer words. The therapist needs the capacity to be receptive to the client's projected feelings without being overwhelmed by them, or being driven to repudiate the feelings and push them back into the client. The therapist needs to be able to stand back and disentangle his or her feelings which may be mobilised by the client from feelings the therapist may want to project into the client. The feelings may be mobilised unconsciously by the client with the hope that such feelings will be understood, or there may be a wish in phantasy to evacuate the feelings. Nonetheless, the therapist's receptivity to such projective processes provides important clues for understanding more about the client's unconscious states of mind.

The capacity to extract oneself from a delusional merger with the client essentially comes from one's understanding and knowledge of a body of theory and practice, personal therapy and, especially supervision. For example it is a familiar experience in supervision to become aware of something that seems obvious to others and yet one was unable to see at the time (Caper, 1999). Supervision, or one's relationship to a body of theory provides another perspective which helps prise apart the merged couple of therapist and client; and provides a means of thinking about and bearing what may be experienced as unthinkable and unbearable. If the therapist can contain these feelings then the client can have some hope that at the very least there is someone who can bear the feelings, think about and try to make sense of the unthinkable aspects of their experience. Some clients may have suffered too much emotional damage, may not have sufficient emotional resources to establish an inner sense of containment and may always need some kind of external source of containment. Some clients may for a long time need an external person in order to feel understood, and may only very gradually develop a capacity to understand (Steiner, 1993). With repeated experiences of containment the client may eventually be able to retrieve these lost aspects of the self, feel more integrated and whole.

In the case of Mr Stringer, who was suffering from dementia and the terrors of losing his mind, it seemed that Dominik's willingness to sit with him and try to think about Mr Stringer's experience facilitated a friendly contact and a hope that Dominik might understand something about a frightening disability. Perhaps what was also projected was the difficulty, even terror in thinking about this disability and where it would lead.

Mrs King's apparently helpful advice to Dominik that he should take up swimming to straighten himself out was a cruel attack which gave him some experience of her internal world. I suspect that what was externalised in this attack on Dominik was how a psychotic, destructive part of her mind attacks her vulnerable and dependent self, but deceptively, in way which could appear helpful (Steiner, 1993). It is this untrustworthy part of her mind which was projected into doctors and nurses who were trying to help her. Her vulnerable self was persuaded that it was the staff who were untrustworthy through propaganda which was used to obstruct access to their help. Similarly, when Gary was with Mrs Rice and felt as if he was dragging a lamb to the slaughter, I think he received some of the projected cruelty of the destructive psychotic aspect of her personality which prevented her dependent self receiving the help it so desperately needed, and which murderously attacked her in the suicide attempt. Her vulnerable self was persuaded that it was Gary who was cruel and dragging her to destruction.

When Michele felt so guilty about not being able to bear taking Mrs Holly on for counselling, I think she received a projected aspect of a severe and ruthless super-ego. When I discussed this guilt with Michele and offered a more sympathetic and realistic perspective which recognised our ordinary limits and vulnerabilities, this eased the guilt and what had to be borne. I think Mrs Holly's many tragedies and problems were made more difficult for her to bear by a savage super-ego masquerading as a conscience which blamed her and made her feel guilty for much of what happened to her, as though, as she said, she were burning in hell.

In supervision helping the trainees understand and process their emotional experiences with the clients enables them to feel that their own worries and vulnerabilities can be held and in turn helps them hold their clients. The focus of the therapeutic work may, for a long time, be on offering supportive therapy in which the trainee learns to recognise unconscious communication and monitor it, but does not attempt to bring the unconscious into consciousness by interpreting. This work aims to help the trainee provide greater understanding and containment for the client's conscious and unconscious feelings, without any expectation that the client will be able to retrieve projected aspects of him- or herself.

When a trainee begins to work interpretatively the emphasis is to offer what John Steiner (1993) calls 'analyst centred interpretations' which is to describe the client's unconscious experience of the therapist and not to point out what the client might be doing to the therapist. Such interpretations aim to articulate the nature of the projections in the transference and the resulting way the therapist is experienced which demonstrates that the projections can be borne and thought about by someone else. Eventually the client may be enabled to retrieve the projected aspects of him- or herself through the work of mourning to help the client separate from the therapist, especially by attending to the client's feelings about separations, whether at the endings of sessions, holidays and absences, and finally the termination of the therapy.

## Summary

Monitoring one's own emotional responses – the counter-transference – is central to contemporary psychodynamic practice and to teaching and learning about psychodynamic therapy with older people. The centrality of counter-transference reflects the understanding of the communicative aspects of projective identification. Observational studies, by virtue of freeing the trainees of the responsibility of making a therapeutic intervention, help trainees to become more sensitive to their own emotional responses, to sustain feelings rather than discharge them in actions and to learn how reflecting on their emotional reactions may inform their understanding about their clients. Like all of us, trainees bring their own vulnerabilities to which clients can be acutely sensitive and may hook into for purposes of projective identification. An important part of the supervisory process is containing the trainee's anxiety and helping him or her to be receptive to the client's unconscious use of the trainee's anxieties and vulnerabilities and to understand the communicative aspects of this projective process. Reflecting on counter-transference reactions is crucial in learning about psychodynamic therapy, and can be particularly useful in working with people suffering from dementia for whom other forms of communication may no longer be possible.

Growing old confronts us with our physical and mental vulnerabilities as our bodies and brains wear out. Above all we are confronted with the limits of life itself as we face the deaths of contemporaries, family and friends, and ultimately the end of our own lives. Limits and vulnerability are not confined to the old. Trainees, because of their fledgling state, are likely to feel especially vulnerable and worried, and thereby present ready hooks for projective communications about vulnerability. If their own worries are adequately supported they are then in a stronger position to be receptive to the projected feelings stirred in them and may gain some insight into the internal difficulties which can make aspects of ageing and dying so very troublesome. These internal difficulties may be an intolerance of dependency and neediness which comes from psychotic, narcissistic or omnipotent aspects of the mind. This can be played out in the therapeutic relationship where the therapist is the recipient for the client's projected dependent and vulnerable self. As such, the therapist carries the hope for helping this self and at the same time may have to bear abuse and hatred from other parts of the client's personality for which such vulnerability is intolerable. Such intolerances may stem from earlier failed dependency relationships or other environmental or constitutional factors, but what becomes available for understanding through the therapist's feelings are communications in the here-and-now of the therapeutic relationship about such enduring fears.

The therapeutic relationship offers containment for fears of dependency and vulnerability because the therapist aims to be someone who can be depended upon to receive projected, unmanageable aspects of the client. Some older clients may never be able to retrieve the projections but at least may feel contained. Other older clients may come to feel more complete and integrated through the therapeutic work of mourning. Thus the ending of this book returns to its beginning in recognising the importance of mourning in therapy with older people.

# REFERENCES

D. Atkins and D. Loewenthal (2004) 'The lived experience of psychotherapists working with older clients: an heuristic study', *British Journal of Guidance and Counselling*, 32, 4, 493–509.

E. Bick (1968) 'The experience of the skin in early object relations' in E. Bott-Spillius (ed.) *Melanie Klein To-day Volume 1* (London: Routledge, 1988), pp. 187–91.

J. Bicknell (1983) 'The psychopathology of handicap', *British Journal of Medical Psychology*, 56, 167–78.

S. Biggs (1989) 'Professional Helpers and Resistances to Work with Older People', *Ageing and Society*, 9, 43–60.

W.R. Bion (1959) 'Attacks on linking', *International Journal of Psycho-analysis*, 40, 308–15.

W.R. Bion (1962) 'A theory of thinking' in E. Bott-Spillius (ed.) *Melanie Klein To-day Volume 1* (London: Routledge, 1988), pp. 178–86.

W. Bolton and V. Zagier Roberts (1994) 'Asking for help: staff support and sensitivity groups reviewed' in A. Obholzer and V. Zagier Roberts (eds) *The Unconscious at Work* (London: Routledge, 1994), pp. 156–69.

I. Brenman Pick (1985) 'Working through in the counter-transference' in E. Bott-Spillius (ed.) *Melanie Klein To-day Volume 1* (London: Routledge, 1988), pp. 34–47.

R. Britton (1989) 'The missing link: parental sexuality in the Oedipus complex' in Britton, R. et al *The Oedipus Complex Today* (London: Karnac).

R. Caper (1999) *A Mind of One's Own* (London: Routledge).

R. Caper (2000) *Immaterial Facts* (London: Routledge).

P. Clark and A. Bowling (1989) 'Observational Study of Quality of Life in NHS Nursing Homes and a Long-stay Ward for the Elderly', *Ageing and Society*, 9, 123–48.

E. Cleavely (1993) 'Relationships: interaction, defences, and transformations' in S. Ruszczynski (ed.) *Psychotherapy with Couples* (London: Karnac), pp. 56–69.

K. Codeco Barone (2005) 'On the process of working through caused by severe illnesses in childhood: A psychoanalytical approach', *Psychoanalytic Psychotherapy*, 19, 1, 17–34.

W. Colman (1993) 'Marriage as a psychological container' in S. Ruszczynski (ed.) *Psychotherapy with Couples* (London: Karnac), pp. 70–98.

S. Critchley-Robbins (2004) 'Brief Psychodynamic Therapy with Older People' in S. Evans and J. Garner (eds) *Talking Over the Years* (London: Brunner Routledge), pp. 147–64.

A. Dartington (1994) 'Where Angels fear to Tread' in A. Obholzer and V. Zagier Roberts (eds) *The Unconscious at Work* (London: Routledge, 1994), pp. 101–9.

T. Dartington (1993) 'Clinical Commentary XVI', *British Journal of Psychotherapy*, 10, 2, 258–69.

R. Davenhill (2007a) 'Developments in psychoanalytic thinking and in therapeutic attitudes and services' in R. Davenhill (ed.) *Looking into Later Life* (London: Karnac), pp. 11–31.

R. Davenhill (2007b) 'No truce with the furies: issues of containment in the provision of care for older people with dementia and those who care for them' in R. Davenhill (ed.) *Looking into Later Life* (London: Karnac), pp. 201–21.

R. Davenhill, A. Balfour and M. Rustin (2007) 'Psychodynamic Observation and Old Age' in R. Davenhill (ed.) *Looking into Later Life* (London: Karnac), pp. 129–44.

S. de Beauvoir (1970) *Old Age* (Harmondsworth: Penguin).

F. De Masi (2004) *Making Death Thinkable* (London: Free Association).

M. Dennis and D. Armstrong (2007) 'Consultation at work' in R. Davenhill (ed.) *Looking into Later Life* (London: Karnac), pp. 145–59.

M. Eastman (1993) 'Elder Abuse, Education and Training' in Review Symposium, *Ageing and Society*, 13, 1, 115–17.

S. Evans (2004a) 'Elderly couples and their families' in S. Evans and J. Garner (eds) *Talking Over the Years* (London: Brunner Routledge), pp. 211–46.

S. Evans (2004b) 'Group psychotherapy: Foulkes, Yalom and Bion' in S. Evans and J. Garner (eds) *Talking Over the Years* (London: Brunner Routledge), pp. 87–100.

J. Fisher (1993) 'The impenetrable other: ambivalence and the Oedipal conflict in work with couples' in S. Ruszczynski (ed.) *Psychotherapy with Couples* (London: Karnac), pp. 142–66.

J. Fisher (1995) 'Identity and Intimacy in the couple: three kinds of identification' in S. Ruszczynski and J. Fisher (eds) *Intrusiveness and Intimacy in the Couple* (London: Karnac), pp. 74–104.

S. Freud (1917) 'Mourning and Melancholia', *Standard Edition*, 11 (London: Hogarth).

S. Freud (1896) 'Further remarks on the neuro-psychoses of defence', *Standard Edition*, 3 (London: Hogarth).

S. Freud (1905a) 'Fragment of an analysis of a case of hysteria', *Standard Edition*, 7 (London: Hogarth).

S. Freud (1905b) 'On Psychotherapy', *Standard Edition*, 7 (London: Hogarth).

S. Freud (1914) 'Remembering, repeating and working through', *Standard Edition*, 12 (London: Hogarth).

C. Garland (1991) 'External disasters and the internal world: an approach to psycho-therapeutic understanding of survivors' in J. Holmes (ed.) *Textbook of Psychotherapy in Psychiatric Practice* (London: Churchill Livingstone), pp. 507–32.

C. Garland (2007) 'Tragi-comical-historical-pastoral: groups and group therapy in the third age' in R. Davenhill (ed.) *Looking into Later Life* (London: Karnac), pp. 90–107.

J. Garner (2004) 'Dementia' in S. Evans and J. Garner (eds) *Talking Over the Years* (London: Brunner Routledge), pp. 131–46.

F. Glendenning (1993) 'Elder Abuse, Education and Training' in Review Symposium, *Ageing and Society*, 13, 1, 117–21.

P. Heimann (1950) 'On counter-transference', *International Journal of Psycho-analysis*, 31, 81–4.

N. Hess (1987) 'King Lear and some anxieties of old age', *British Journal of Medical Psychology*, 60, 209–16.

N. Hess (2001) 'The function and value of staff groups on psychiatric wards', *Psychoanalytic Psychotherapy*, 15, 2, 121–30.

N. Hess (2004) 'Loneliness in Old Age: Klein and others' in S. Evans and J. Garner (eds) *Talking Over the Years* (London: Brunner Routledge), pp. 19–28.

P. Hildebrand (1995) *Beyond Mid-Life Crisis* (London: Sheldon Press).

R.D. Hinshelwood (1987) *What Happens in Groups* (London: Free Association Books).

R.D. Hinshelwood (2002) 'Psychological defence and nuclear war' in Covington C. et al (eds) *Terrorism and War* (London: Karnac).

E. Hinze (1987) 'Transference, countertransference in the psychoanalytic treatment of older patients', *International Review of Psycho-analysis*, 14, 465–74.

E. Jaques (1965) 'Death and the mid-life crisis' in E. Bott-Spillius (ed.) *Melanie Klein To-day Volume 2* (London: Routledge, 1988), pp. 226–48.

D. Judd (1989) *Give Sorrow Words* (London: Free Association).

P. King (1980) 'The Life Cycle as Indicated by the Nature of the Transference in the Psychoanalysis of the Middle-Aged and Elderly', *International Journal of Psycho-Analysis*, 61, 153–60.

M. Klein (1940) 'Mourning and its Relation to Manic-Depressive States' in *The Writings of Melanie Klein Volume I* (London: Hogarth, 1975), pp. 344–79.

M. Klein (1946) 'Notes on Some Schizoid Mechanisms' in *The Writings of Melanie Klein Volume III* (London: Hogarth, 1975), pp. 1–24.

K. Lee, P.J. Volans and N. Gregory (2003) 'Trainee clinical psychologists' views on recruitment to work with older people', *Ageing and Society*, 23, 83–97.

D. Lessing (1984) *The Diaries of Jane Sommers* (Harmondsworth: Penguin).

M. Likierman (2001) *Melanie Klein: her work in context* (London: Continuum).

B. Martindale (1989a) 'Becoming Dependent Again', *Psychoanalytic Psychotherapy*, 4, 67–75.

B. Martindale (1989b) 'Review of Group Psychotherapies for the Elderly', *International Review of Psycho-Analysis*, 16, 508–10.

B. Martindale (2007) 'Resilience and Vulnerability in Later Life', *British Journal of Psychotherapy*, 23, 2, 205–16.

A. Mason (1981) 'The Suffocating Super-Ego: Psychotic Breaks and Claustrophobia' in J. Grotstein (ed.) *Do I Dare Disturb the Universe* (London: Karnac), pp. 139–66.

K. McHugh (2003) 'Three faces of ageism: society, image and place', *Ageing and Society*, 23, 165–85.

S. McKenzie-Smith (1992) 'A psycho-analytical study of the elderly', *Free Associations*, 27, 3, 3, 355–91.

D. Meltzer and M. Harris Williams (1988) *The Apprehension of Beauty* (Strath Tay, Perthshire: Clunies Press).

I. Menzies-Lyth (1960) *Social Systems as a Defence Against Anxiety* (London: Tavistock Institute of Human Relations, 1970).

E.J. Miller and G.V. Gwynne (1973) 'Dependence, independence and counter-dependence in residential institutions for incurables' in E.J. Miller, *From Dependency to Autonomy* (London: Free Association, 1993), pp. 67–81.

J. Milton (1994) 'Abuser and Abused: perverse solutions following childhood abuse', *Psychoanalytic Psychotherapy*, 8, 3, 243–55.

F. Morante (2005) 'Applying psychoanalytic thinking in a staff support group to reflect on service change and clinical practice in a specialist psychiatric service', *Psychoanalytic Psychotherapy*, 19, 2, 103–20.

B. Morrison (2006) 'I said to the nurse, please feed her', *The Guardian*, 7/01/06, available at http://www.guardian.co.uk/family/story/0,,1680652,00.html

M. Nolan (1993) 'Carer-Dependant Relationships and the Prevention of Elder Abuse' in P. Declamer and F. Glendenning (eds) *The Mistreatment of Elderly People* (London: Sage), pp. 148–58.

E. Noonan (1983) *Counselling Young People* (London: Routledge).

E. O'Shaughnessy (1999) 'Relating To The Superego', *International Journal of Psycho-analysis*, 80, 5, 861–70.

G. Pasquali (1993) 'On separateness', *Psychoanalytic Psychotherapy*, 7, 2, 181–91.

F. Plotkin (2000) 'Treatment of the older adult: the impact on the psychoanalyst', *Journal of American Psychoanalytical Association*, 48, 1591–616.

R. Porter (1991) 'Psychotherapy with the elderly' in J. Holmes (ed.) *Textbook of Psychotherapy in Psychiatric Practice* (London: Churchill Livingstone), pp. 469–88.

J. Reggiori (2004) 'Individual psychotherapy in the second half of life' in S. Evans and J. Garner (eds) *Talking Over the Years* (London: Brunner Routledge), pp. 131–46.

I. Robbins (1994) 'The long term psychological effects of the civilian evacuations in World War Two Britain', *British Psychological Society PSIGE Newsletter*, 48, 29–31.

S. Robertson and S. Davison (1997) 'A Survey of Groups within a Psychiatric Hospital', *Psychoanalytic Psychotherapy*, 11, 2, 119–34.

M. Rustin (1989) 'Observing Infants: Reflections on Methods' in L. Miller, et al (eds) *Closely Observed Infants* (London: Duckworth), pp. 52–78.

S. Ruszczynski (1993) 'Thinking about and working with couples' in S. Ruszczynski (ed.) *Psychotherapy with Couples* (London: Karnac), pp. 197–217.

H. Segal (1986) 'Fear of death: notes on the analysis of an old man' in *The Work of Hanna Segal* (London: Free Association), pp. 173–84.

V. Sinason (1986) 'Secondary mental handicap and its relation to trauma', *Psychoanalytic Psychotherapy*, 2, 131–54.

V. Sinason (1988) 'Smiling, swallowing, sickening and stupefying: the effect of sexual abuse on the child', *Psychoanalytic Psychotherapy*, 3, 2, 97–112.

V. Sinason (1992) *Mental Handicap and The Human Condition* (London: Free Association).

J. Steiner (1989) 'The aim of psychoanalysis', *Psychoanalytic Psychotherapy*, 4, 2, 109–20.

J. Steiner (1993) *Psychic Retreats* (London: Routledge).

P. Speck (1994) 'Working with dying people: on being good enough' in A. Obholzer and V. Zagier Roberts (eds) *The Unconscious at Work* (London: Routledge, 1994), pp. 94–100.

J. Symington (1985) 'The Survival Function of Primitive Omnipotence', *International Journal of Psycho-analysis*, 66, 481–7.

N. Symington (2001) *The Spirit of Sanity* (London: Karnac).

P. Terry (1998) 'Who will care for the older people? – A case study of working with destructiveness and despair in long stay care', *Journal of Social Work Practice*, 12, 2, 209–16.

P. Terry (2006) 'Terrors of Growing Old: Dependency, Loneliness and Death', *Therapy Today*, 17, 3, 9–11.

R.M. Young (1995) 'The vicissitudes of transference and counter-transference: The work of Harold Searles', *Free Associations*, 5, 2, 171–95.

J. Werth, K. Kopera-Frye, D. Blevins and B. Bossick (2003) 'Older Adult Representation in the Counselling Psychology Literature', *The Counselling Psychologist*, 31, 6, 789–814.

H.W. Wylie (1987) 'The older analysand: countertransference issues in psycho-analysis', *International Journal of Psycho-analysis*, 68, 343–52.

V. Zagier Roberts (1994) 'Till death do us part: caring and uncaring in work with the elderly' in A. Obholzer and V. Zagier Roberts (eds) *The Unconscious at Work* (London: Routledge, 1994), pp. 75–83.

# INDEX

Symington, J.   x, 41, 117
Symington, N.   114

Terry, P.   92, 114, 121
trainee therapists, supervision of
    *see* Chapter 10
transference   11, 28–9, 40–1, 50, 78,
    85–6
  and couple therapy   72, 78
  and support groups   139–40, 147
  split   29–30, 40, 42
tyranny, and control in older
    people   118

unconscious phantasy   6
unintegration and fears of being
    unheld   37, 117, 122–3

war, and post-traumatic stress   50
'warehousing ideology' in caring
    institutions   94
Werth, J. et al   121
Wylie, H.W.   122

Young, R.   55

Zagier Roberts, V.   65